Pelican Books
Tao: *The Watercourse Way*

During the past thirty years Alan Watts became known
through his many books as one of the most stimulating
and unconventional philosophers of our time. He
published over a dozen books on comparative
philosophy and religion and was well known in the
United States as a lecturer and teacher. He specialized
in the interpretation of Eastern thought to the
West, and particularly of the type of Buddhism
known as Zen. In his last book, *Tao: The Watercourse,
Way*, Alan Watts turns his attention to the Chinese
philosophy of the Tao, treating the material much as
he did for Zen Buddhism in his classic *The Way
of Zen* (also in Pelican).

Alan Watts was born in England and went to the
States in 1938, becoming in turn editor, minister
and college professor. He was guest lecturer at
Cambridge, Cornell, and Hawaii, and for some time
was a religious counsellor at Northwestern University.
He also spoke before the American Psychiatric
Association, the C. G. Jung Institute in Zurich,
and the medical staffs of American hospitals. He
then became Dean of the American Academy of Asian
Studies in San Francisco. Alan Watts died in 1973.

# TAO: *The Watercourse Way*

## ALAN WATTS

WITH THE COLLABORATION OF
## AL CHUNG-LIANG HUANG

*Additional calligraphy by Lee Chih-chang*

**Penguin Books Ltd, Harmondsworth, Middlesex, England**
Penguin Books, 625 Madison Avenue, New York, New York 10022, U.S.A.
Penguin Books Australia Ltd, Ringwood, Victoria, Australia
Penguin Books Canada Ltd, 2801 John Street, Markham, Ontario, Canada L3R 1B4
Penguin Books (N.Z.) Ltd, 182–190 Wairau Road, Auckland 10, New Zealand

First published in the U.S.A. 1975
Published in Great Britain by Jonathan Cape 1976
Published in Pelican Books 1979

Grateful acknowledgement is made to the following for permission to reprint
previously published material:

George Allen & Unwin Ltd with the approval of the Buddhist Society, London:
Excerpts (some slightly modified) from *Tao Te Ching* by Lao-tzu, translated by
Ch'u Ta-kao, 1939.

AMS Press, Inc.: Excerpts from *Chuang Tzu: Mystic, Moralist, and Social Planner*, by
Chuang Tzu, translated from the Chinese by Herbert A. Giles. Second edition, revised,
published by AMS Press, Inc., N.Y., 1972. Originally published by Kelly and Walsh,
Shanghai, 1926.

Columbia University Press: Excerpts from pages 108–9, 182, 209–210, 216 of
*The Complete Works of Chuang Tzu*, translated by Burton Watson. Columbia University
Press, 1968.

Alfred A. Knopf, Inc.: Excerpt (slightly modified) fom *Tao Te Ching* by Lao Tzu,
translated by Gia-fu Feng and Jane English, Copyright © 1972 by Gia-fu Feng and Jane
English; and one excerpt from *Chuang Tsu: Inner Chapters*, translated by Gia-fu Feng and
Jane English, Copyright © 1974 by Gia-fu Feng and Jane English.

Paragon Book Gallery, Ltd.: Excerpts (some slightly modifed) from *Chuang-Tzu:
A New Selected Translation*, by Fung Yu-lan, reprinted by Paragon Book Reprint Corp.,
1963.

Princeton University Press: Quotation from *The I Ching: Or Book of Changes*,
translated by Richard Wilhelm, rendered into English by Cary F. Baynes,
Bollingen Series XIX, Copyright 1950, © 1967 by Bollingen Foundation; and
selections from pages 166–167, 177 of Vol. I, *The Period of the Philosophers from the
the Beginnings to circa 100 B.C.* in Fung Yu-lan, *A History of Chinese Philosophy*,
translated by Derk Bodde, Princeton University Press, 1952.

Design by Kenneth Miyamoto

Made and printed in Great Britain by
Richard Clay (The Chaucer Press) Ltd
Bungay, Suffolk
Set in Monotype Times

# Contents

# Foreword

Al Chung-liang Huang

THE LAST MORNING I was with Alan Watts was spent in his mountain library overlooking Muir Woods, drinking tea, playing a bamboo flute, and plucking koto strings among the eucalyptus. We had just taught for a week together at Esalen Institute, Big Sur, and on the ferryboat of the Society for Comparative Philosophy in Sausalito. I was helping him with research on his book, and he had just finished reading the manuscript of my book, *Embrace Tiger, Return to Mountain*. We were sitting on the library floor, comparing notes, nodding, smiling. Suddenly Alan jumped to his feet and joyously danced a *t'ai chi* improvisation, shouting, "Ah-ha, *t'ai chi* is the Tao, *wu-wei*, *tzu-jan*, like water, like wind, sailing, surfing, dancing with your hands, your head, your spine, your hips, your knees . . . with your brush, your voice . . . Ha Ha ha Ha . . . La La Lala ah ah Ah . . ." Gracefully he glided into the desk seat, rolled a sheet of paper into the typewriter, and began dancing with his fingers, still singing away. He was writing a foreword for my book, composing a beautiful introduction to the essence of *t'ai chi*. It was probably one of his last actual writings before a strenuous European lecture tour took him away from his desk and from his new ways of spontaneous, joyous writing.

Alan was going to allow his book on Taoism to write itself. He knew, as a scholar, that he was turning out another of his famous themes-and-variations on the meeting of East and West. But as a man of Tao, he also realized that he must give up controlling it intellectually. For as the subject itself clearly maintains, "The Tao that can be Tao-ed is not the Tao."

After so many years of writing beautifully the unwritable, Alan Watts was finally stepping aside, letting his writing happen. He turned to me for reflections. He wished to tune in body and mind totally with the movement of the Tao, in *t'ai chi*. Alan was enjoying his newfound energy. He wrote the first five chapters with a great sense of discovery, lucidity, and creative insight. All of us who shared in the progress of this book felt confident that it would be his best, surely the most alive and useful. We could not wait for him to finish it.

From the beginning I had felt honored and happy to be of help to him. Alan was especially interested in the ways I read the original Chinese texts. We both found excitement in deciphering the difficult passages, loaded with ambiguity and multiple interpretative possibilities. We would look at all the existing translations, debate, digest, and dismiss them, and then start afresh, attempting a new, on-the-spot translation to satisfy us.

Alan helped me to feel at ease with my lack of fluency in the English language. He said to me often that my broken Chinese-English rendered the Chinese philosophy more explicitly, and that I must not try so hard to improve it. As a teaching team we complemented each other. We were an ideal combination to help people experience what they think they know—taking them out of their heads into their bodies, then back again into their body-mind entity. Finally, Alan asked me to illustrate the book entirely with brush calligraphy. We agreed that the free-flowing brush strokes of the cursive (grass style) would most vividly bring out the watercourse way of the Tao.

After he had finished the chapter "*Te*—Virtuality," Alan said to me with a special glint in his eyes, "I have now satisfied myself and my readers in scholarship and intellect. The rest of this book will be all fun and surprises!" Alan had hoped to bring the Tao to his readers the way he practiced and experienced it in everyday living. Many new vistas had opened in Alan's life. He was like a child again, willing and able to set forth upon new courses and follow the inevitable turning of energies.

During our last seminar at Esalen together, at the finish of an afternoon session when the high-flying spirit had set everyone smiling, dancing, and rolling up and down the grassy slopes, Alan and I started to walk back to the lodge, feeling exuberant, arms around each other, hands sliding along one another's spine. Alan turned to me and started to speak, ready to impress me with his usual eloquence about our successful week together. I noticed a sudden breakthrough in his expression; a look of lightness and glow appeared all around him. Alan had discovered a different way to tell me of his feelings: "Yah . . . Ha . . . Ho . . . Ha! Ho . . . La Cha Om Ha . . . Deg deg te te . . . Ta De De Ta Te Ta . . . Ha Te Te Ha Hom . . . Te Te Te . . ." We gibbered and danced all the way up the hill. Everyone around understood what we were saying. Alan knew too that he had never—not in all his books —said it any better than that.

At the Alan Watts memorial celebration in the Palace of Fine Arts in San Francisco, someone in the audience shouted to Jano Watts: "What was it like to live with Alan?" Her answer: "Never dull. He was a man full of fun and surprises. And the biggest surprise of all was on November sixteenth last year." During that last evening of his life Alan Watts played with balloons. He described the weightless, floating sensation as being "like my spirit leaving my body." In the night he went on to a new journey of the spirit, riding the wind, laughing joyously.

He left behind, us, the living, missing him terribly for his bravura human aliveness. He left also empty pages, a proposed two more chapters of "fun and surprises" of the book he had begun on the Tao. Many of us with whom he discussed this work, or who met with him during the summerlong seminars on Taoism while *The Watercourse Way* was happening, knew that in the final two chapters of the intended seven Alan hoped to let it be seen how the ancient, timeless Chinese wisdom was medicine for the ills of the West. Yet, paradoxically, it must not be taken as medicine, an intellectually swallowed "pill," but allowed joyously to infuse our total being and so transform our individual lives and through them our society.

Elsa Gidlow, Alan's longtime friend and neighbor, discussed this with me often. She confirmed our talks by writing the following:

> It was his vision that modern technological man, in attempting absolute control over nature (from which he tended to see himself divided) and over all the uses of human society, was caught in a trap, himself becoming enslaved. Every control requires further control until the "controller" himself is enmeshed. Alan was fond of pointing to Lao-tzu's counsel to the emperors: "Govern a large country as you would cook a small fish: lightly." But it should be understood that Alan never saw "the watercourse way" in human affairs as a flabby, irresponsible, lackadaisical manner of living. The stream does not merely move downhill. The water, all moisture, transpires from the earth, streams, rivers, the ocean, to the upper air, a "breathing out," and then there is the "breathing in" when the moisture is returned downward as dew, as rain—a marvelous cycle, a living interaction: nothing controlling anything, no "boss," yet all happening as it should, *tse jen*.

Just how Alan would have communicated in his final

chapters his insights into the need of the West for a realization and a living of the Way of the Tao, we can only guess. What we do know is that it transformed him as he allowed it to permeate his being, so that the reserved, somewhat uptight young Englishman, living overmuch in his head, in his mature years became an outgoing, spontaneously playful, joyous world sage. He believed that a widespread absorption of the profound wisdom of Taoism could similarly transform the West. This book was to be his contribution to the process.

So, when all fingers pointed toward me to undertake completion of this book, I realized that I must not try to imitate Alan or get into his mind, but attempt to show, from my knowing him, where he had arrived. My initial thoughts were sentimental and tributary. I began to relive my memories of Alan Watts. I wanted to share with the readers the total man Alan, not just his brains and words. I wrote about our first meeting dancing on the beach at Santa Barbara, our first Oriental meal together when Alan spoke more Japanese than I. I wrote about exciting events and moments in our many joint seminars which clearly demonstrated Alan's natural Tao as teacher-man.

I remembered one New Year's Eve celebration when we inspired a blind drummer to beat out the rhythm of our cursive, calligraphic dialogue. How everyone picked up the splash-splatter motions of our ink brushes and began dancing spontaneously their own individual body-brush strokes. Another time when Alan and I guided a blind girl into our mind-body by touching and moving with her so she could gradually see and feel through her inner visions. I recalled rituals and games we played: weddings conducted out of rigid procedures into a true spirit of love and union; impromptu *chanoyu* or tea ceremonies with unauthentic equipment, yet performed and observed in reverent essence.

Alan Watts was a philosophical entertainer. He knew himself to be so. His foremost concern was enjoyment for himself and for his audience. He easily lifted the usual academic seriousness, along with dutiful learning, to new and higher planes of joyous playfulness in natural growth.

And yet, all this remembrance is only thoughts of the past. What is happening to Alan now? What are his current, on-going "fun and surprises"?

On New Year's Eve 1973–4, during Alan's forty-nine-days' Bardo Journey (the Tibetan and Chinese concept of the intermediate stages between death and rebirth) and only a few days before his fifty-eighth birthday, I had an unusual dream about juxtaposed time-space-people. It was in China, I thought, during a chanting session with the monks for my father's Bardo. Then the place became Alan's circular library where Alan himself was conducting the service, speaking in my father's voice in Chinese. I was playing the flute, but the sound I made was that of a gong, mixed with beats of the woodblock. Then Alan changed into my father, speaking an unrecognizable yet perfectly intelligible language. The boom-ing, resonating voice gradually became the sound of the bamboo flute I was playing, reading his lips. My vision zoomed close to the dark moving void between the lips, entering into a sound chamber swirling with colors and lights, deeper and deeper into the stillness of the continuing sound of the bam-boo. I woke up not knowing who, when, or where I was. Next thing, I was flying in the sky (was it by plane?) to arrive at Alan's library by midday New Year's.

For the first time since his passing in November I felt I was truly close to him. Sitting on the deck outside the picture window before which Alan's ashes rested on the altar, I let the sound of my bamboo flute echo over the valley and hills.

It was a clear and beautiful day. Later, I put on Jano's climbing shoes, threw a blanket wrap over my neck, took Alan's Tibetan walking staff, and walked down the small path into the depth of the woods. The sound of the bamboo carried everything inside me to Alan, to everything that is the these far-off echoes of philosophy mean to me and to our own historical situation. In other words, there is a value in the effort to find out what did, in fact, happen in remote times and to master the details of philology. But what then? Having done as well as we can to record the past we must go on to make use of it in our present context, and this is my main interest in writing this book. I want to interpret and clarify the principles of such writings as the *Lao-tzu, Chuang-tzu,* 子 and *Lieh-tzu* books in the terms and ideas of our own day, while giving the original texts as accurately translated as possible—that is, without undue paraphrase or poetic elaboration, following the principles of that master translator Arthur Waley, though with some minor reservations.

老子 莊子

It will be obvious that I am heavily indebted to the work and the methods of Joseph Needham and his collaborators at Cambridge University in the production of the many-volumed *Science and Civilization in China,* and though I am not regarding this work as if it were the voice of God, it is, for me, the most marvelous historical enterprise of this century. Needham has the knack of putting out fully documented scholarship as readable as a novel, and, both through reading his work and through personal conversation, my understanding of the Tao has been greatly clarified. He also understands that writing history and philosophy is, like research in science, a social undertaking, so that his work is somewhat more of a conducted chorus than a solo. I think it unfortunate that, especially in America, Sinologists tend to be cantankerous, and hypercritical of each other's work. Needham, on the other hand, is invariably generous without surrender of his own integrity, and I shall try, in what follows, to show how the principle of the Tao reconciles sociability with individuality, order with spontaneity, and unity with diversity.

In sum, I am not attempting to conduct a popular and statistically accurate poll of what Chinese people did, or now do, suppose the Taoist way of life to be. Such meticulous explorations of cultural anthropology have their virtue, but I am much more interested in how these ancient writings reverberate on the harp of my own brain, which has, of course, been tuned to the scales of Western culture. Although I will by no means despise precise and descriptive information—the Letter, I am obviously more interested in the Spirit—the actual experiencing and feeling of that attitude to life which is the following of the Tao.

A.W.

# Prolegomena

---

## BIBLIOGRAPHY

TO AVOID TIRESOME FOOTNOTATION, bibliographical references to Western sources are simply indicated as, e.g., "H. A. Giles (1)" or "Legge (2)," so that by name and number a detailed identification of works consulted may be found in the Bibliography. There is a separate bibliography for original Chinese sources, and the references to these are italicized, as *Chuang-tzu* 12. The Chinese ideograms for brief words and phrases are printed in the margin alongside their romanized forms. On pages 56–73 and 99–104, many of the quotations from Chinese sources are given in Chinese calligraphy. The special importance of including Chinese ideograms is explained in the first chapter in such a way, I trust, that even the nonscholar will find it helpful.

## TRANSLATION

I must admit right here that I am by no means such a scholar and interpreter of the Chinese language as Giles, Waley, Demiéville, Hurwitz, Bodde, Watson, or Needham—not to mention such Chinese masters of English as Hu Shih and Lin

Yutang. But I have the nerve to believe that I understand the basic principles of Taoism more thoroughly than some scholars whose interest is narrowly philological. Thus when a translation is by someone else it is identified as, e.g., "tr. Lin Yutang (1)." When I have compared several translations of a passage and made up my own mind as to how it should go it is identified as, e.g., "tr. Watson (1), mod. auct." When it is simply my own it is identified as "tr. auct." I must confess to a sentimental liking for such Latinisms, along with such others as *ibid.*, [*sic*], *q.v.*, *et seq.*, and *e.g.*, which conveniently abbreviate their drawn-out equivalents: "from the same work," or "that, believe it or not, is just what it says," or "refer to the source mentioned," or "and what follows," or "for example." Furthermore, they may be identified in any adequate dictionary of English.

## ROMANIZATION

There is no fully satisfactory way of romanizing either Chinese or Japanese. The word *Tao* will be pronounced approximately as "dow" in Peking, as "toe" in Canton, and as "daw" in Tokyo. But if I were to substitute any one of these three for *Tao* (which, hereafter, will be adopted into the English language and unitalicized), I would simply be behaving freakishly and confusingly in the context of British, American, and much European literature about China. There is also a word romanized as *T'ao* (pronounced in Peking as "tow-" in "towel") which, according to the tone used in uttering the vowel and the context in which it is used, can mean to desire, recklessness, insolence, to doubt, to pull or clean out, to overflow, a sheath or quiver, a sash or cord, gluttony, a peach, profligacy, marriage, to escape, a special type of hand-drum, to weep, to scour, to bind or braid, a kiln for pottery, to be pleased, to beg, to punish or exterminate, a block of wood (as well as a blockhead), great waves, and packaging. Before you condemn this as irrational, consider the number of meanings for the sound "jack" in English—with no tonal alteration to differentiate them. And for almost all the varied meanings of the sound *T'ao* there are distinctly different ideograms.

Throughout the English-speaking world the most usual form of romanizing Chinese is known as the Wade-Giles system, which is explained in a table at the end of this section (p. xxi) because, in spite of its defects, I am going to use it. No uninitiated English-speaking person could guess how to pronounce it, and I have even thought, in a jocularly malicious state of mind, that Professors Wade and Giles invented it so as to erect a barrier between profane and illiterate people and true scholars. As alternatives there are such awkwardnesses as invented by the Reverend Professor James Legge—e.g., Kwang-ℨze for Chuang-tzu—which require a bizarre font of type, and if one is going to resort to weird letters at all, one may just as well use Chinese itself. I have seriously considered using Needham's revision of the Wade-Giles system, which would, for example, substitute *Thao* for *T'ao* and *Chhang* for *Ch'ang*, but I can't help feeling that the apostrophe is less obnoxious, aesthetically, than the double *h* which, furthermore, does not really suggest the difference: that *Chang* is pronounced "jang" and that *Ch'ang* is pronounced "chang," with an "a" sound close to the "u" in the English "jug." Department of utter confusion! In San Francisco's Chinatown they will spell out the Wade-Giles *Feng* as *Fung* (same "u" as in "jug") and *Wang* as *Wong*, so as not to be read as "whang." On the other hand, a restaurant labeled Wooey Looey Gooey is called (to rhyme with "boy") "Woy Loy Goy."

The problem of romanizing ideograms came to an even higher level of comedy when, shortly before World War II, the Japanese government tried to authorize a new *romaiji* in which *Fuji* became *Huzi,* and Prince Chichibu became Prince Titibu, on the principle that the romanization of Japanese should not have been designed solely for English-speaking people. Therefore Germans would certainly have referred to that noble volcano as "Ootzee," while the British and Americans would have sniggered about Prince Titty-boo. Fortunately, the Japanese have dropped this reform, though many Americans go on calling the cities of Kyoto and Hakone "Kigh-oat-oh" and "Hack-own." You should see the complications which come to pass when attempting to romanize even such alphabetic languages as Tibetan or Sanskrit, which seem, from our point of view, languages specifically designed to be difficult. The scholarly establishment has worked it out so that to tell you about the Lord Krishna I must have a typographer who can make it Kṛṣṇa, and to whom does this tell anything, other than those already in the know?[1]

As in some economies the rich keep getting richer and the poor poorer, so in the overspecialized disciplines of modern scholarship the learned get more learned and the ignorant more ignorant—until the two classes can hardly talk to each other. I have dedicated my work to an attempt to bridge this gap, and so now will reveal to the uninitiated the Wade-Giles system of romanizing the Mandarin dialect of Chinese.

官話

[1] I might also have used the somewhat grotesque alphabet of the International Phonetic Symbols, as employed for representing Chinese words in Forrest (1), but then no ordinary reader could make the least sense of it. The problem is really insoluble. I remember that as a small boy I set out to write down everything I knew in such a way as would be intelligible to people living thousands of years hence. But I realized that I must first devise a key-table to the pronunciation of the letters of the alphabet, for which purpose I had to use that same alphabet!

# THE PRONUNCIATION OF CHINESE WORDS

*Consonants*    Aspirated: Read *p'*, *t'*, *k'*, *ch'*, and *ts'* as in
                *p*in, *t*ip, *k*ilt, *ch*in, and bi*ts*.
                Unaspirated: Read *p*, *t*, *k*, *ch*, and *ts* (or *tz*)
                as in *b*in, *d*ip, *g*ilt, *g*in, and bi*ds*.
                *hs* or *sh*, as in *sh*oe.
                *j* is nearly like an "unrolled" *r*, so that *jen* is
                nearly the English *wren*.

*Vowels*        Usually Italian values,
                *a* as in *f*a*ther
                *e* as in *ei*ght
                *eh* as in broth*er*
                *i* as in mach*i*ne and p*i*n
                *ih* as in sh*ir*t
                *o* as in s*o*ap
                *u* as in g*oo*se
                *ü* as in German *ü*ber

*Diphthongs*    *ai* as in l*igh*t
                *ao* as in l*ou*d
                *ei* as in w*eigh*t
                *ia* as in W*illia*m
                *ieh* as in Kor*ea*
                *ou* as in gr*ou*p
                *ua* as in s*wa*n
                *ueh* as in d*oer*
                *ui* as in s*way*
                *uo* as in *whoah!*

*Combinations*  *an* and *ang* as in b*un* and b*ung*
                *en* and *eng* as in wood*en* and am*ong*
                *in* and *ing* as in s*in* and s*ing*
                *un* and *ung* with the *u* as in l*oo*k.

## HISTORICAL NOTES

孔夫子

Until relatively recent times it was generally believed that Lao-tzu was an individual (otherwise known as Lao Tan or Li Erh) who lived at the time of Confucius (K'ung Fu-tzu), that is to say in the —6th and —5th centuries, the assumed dates of Confucius himself being —552 to —479. The name Lao-tzu means the Old Boy, deriving from the legend that he was born with white hair. This date is based on a disputed passage from the historian Ssu-ma Ch'ien (—145 to —79), who relates that Lao-tzu was curator of the royal library at the capital of Lo-yang, where Confucius visited him in —517.

> Li [Lao-tzu] said to K'ung [Confucius]: The men about whom you talk are dead, and their bones are mouldered to dust; only their words are left. Moreover, when the superior man gets his opportunity, he mounts aloft; but when the time is against him, he is carried along by the force of circumstances. I have heard that a good merchant, though he have rich treasures safely stored, appears as if he were poor; and that the superior man, though his virtue be complete, is yet to outward seeming stupid. Put away your proud air and many desires, your insinuating habit and wild will. They are of no advantage to you;—this is all I have to tell you.

After the interview, Confucius is supposed to have said:

> I know how birds can fly, fishes swim, and animals run. But the runner may be snared, the swimmer hooked, and the flyer shot by the arrow. But there is the dragon:—I cannot tell how he mounts on the wind through the clouds, and rises to heaven. Today I have seen Lao-tzu, and can only compare him to the dragon.

To this Ssu-ma Ch'ien adds:

> Lao-tzu cultivated the Tao and its attributes, the chief aim of his studies being how to keep himself concealed and remain unknown. He continued to reside at the capital of Chou, but

after a long time, seeing the decay of the dynasty, he left it and went away to the barrier-gate, leading out of the kingdom on the north-west. Yin Hsi, the warden of the gate, said to him, "You are about to withdraw yourself out of sight. Let me insist on your (first) composing for me a book." On this, Lao-tzu wrote a book in two parts, setting forth his views on the Tao and its attributes, in more than 5000 characters. He then went away, and it is not known where he died. He was a superior man, who liked to keep himself unknown.[2]

In the last fifty years, Chinese, Japanese, and European scholars have, by minute textual criticism, come more or less to the consensus that the *Lao-tzu* book, the *Tao Te Ching*, is a compilation of Taoist sayings by several hands originating in the −4th century, during, and even after, the time of Chuang-tzu, who, according to Fung Yu-lan, must have flourished somewhere between −369 and −286.[3] When I consider the confused opinions arising from textual criticism of the New Testament, I am in some doubt as to how seriously this debunking of the Lao-tzu legend should be taken. Since the latter years of the +19th century, scholars of the Western tradition, including many Chinese and Japanese, seem to have established a trend for casting doubt on the historicity of "legendary" figures of the past—especially if they are of the religious or spiritual type. It will take many years to ascertain whether this is a style or fad of modern scholarship, or honest research. To please their professors, many successful graduate students affect peppery skepticism and an aura of scientific objectivity as a matter of protocol in submitting acceptable dissertations. Because of this way of looking at texts with a big magnifying glass, one sometimes wonders whether pedants miss features which are obvious to the naked eye.

[2] *Shih Chi,* tr. Legge (1), pp. 80–81.
[3] Fung Yu-lan (2), p. 104. For much fuller details on research concerning these dates, see Creel (1), chs. 1 and 4.

To me, the *Tao Te Ching,* the "Book of the Way and Its Power," could very obviously be the work of one hand, allowing for minor interpolations and for such inconsistencies, real or apparent, as may be found in the work of almost any philosopher. Its laconic, aphoristic, and enigmatic style is consistent throughout the book, as is also the very rhythm of its argument: "The Tao is thus and so, and therefore the sage should conduct himself this way and that." By contrast, the style of the *Chuang-tzu* book is entirely different—discursive, argumentative, narrational, and humorous to the point of provoking belly-laughs, so that to one's aesthetic judgment the two books evoke two very different but consistent personalities. As things now stand I do not believe that we know enough about ancient Chinese history and literature to make a firm judgment, and perhaps it will never be possible to do so.

However, the dating of Chuang-tzu (or Chuang-chou) has never been in much dispute, traditionalists and modern scholars both agreeing, in the main, upon the —4th century. He has been related to Lao-tzu as Saint Paul to Jesus, though there is the difference that whereas Saint Paul never quotes the actual words of Jesus, Chuang-tzu quotes Lao-tzu. Lin Yutang's translation of the *Lao-tzu* intersperses its chapters with substantial portions of the *Chuang-tzu* as commentary, and the device works admirably, so that one tends to see in Chuang-tzu a development and elaboration of the pithy thoughts of Lao-tzu.

H. G. Creel says, "The *Chuang-tzu* is in my estimation the finest philosophical work known to me, in any language."[4] The opinion of such a scholar commands respect. Chinese literati likewise feel that its literary style is of superb quality, and there must be many, like myself, who rejoice in Chuang-

[4] Creel (1), p. 55.

tzu as one of the very few philosophers, in all times, who does not take himself painfully seriously, and whose writings are graced with humor of a peculiar character. That is to say, he can laugh about the most profound matters without deriding them, but, on the contrary, making them seem all the more true and profound just because they are comic. Laughter and mysticism, or religion, go together all too rarely. This same attitude may be found, owing, perhaps, to its connections with Taoism, in the literature of Ch'an (Zen) Buddhism, as well as in the personal style of many of its present followers.

There is less assurance as to the dating of the *Lieh-tzu* book. Though assigned by tradition to the —3rd century, it shows the influence of Buddhist ideas, which would suggest a date early in the Christian era, the +1st or +2nd century. Lieh-tzu is also highly critical of what Creel has called "Hsien Taoism," as distinct from "Contemplative Taoism," the former being a quest for immortality and supernormal powers through the gymnosophic and "yogic" practices which seem to have arisen among Taoists in the —2nd and —1st centuries. A *hsien* is an immortal—one who has purified his flesh from decay by special forms of breathing, diet, drugs, and exercises for preserving the semen comparable to those of Tantric Yoga. When his skin grows old and crinkly, he sloughs it like a snake to reveal a youthful body beneath.[5]

仙

The *Huai Nan Tzu* book, which also takes issue with Hsien Taoism, was written under the sponsorship of the Prince of Huai Nan, a relative and vassal of the Emperor Wu named Liu An, and may fairly safely be placed at c. —120. Of this Creel says:

淮南子

[5] See Needham (1), vol. 2, p. 422 and illus. Though the idea is here connected with the Buddhist principle of transformation (*nirmana* or *hua*), I do not find the image of skin-shedding in Indian or Tibetan iconography, and it therefore seems derivative from Hsien Taoism.

化

> A book written under his patronage by various scholars, called the *Huai Nan Tzu,* is eclectic but predominantly Taoist in tone. It contains a good deal of mention of techniques for seeking immortality but never, I believe, recommends them. On the contrary, it insists repeatedly that death and life are just the same, and neither should be sought or feared. It ridicules breath control and gymnastics, which are designed to perpetuate the body but in fact confuse the mind.[6]

The focus of this book is upon Contemplative Taoism rather than Hsien Taoism. I do not know enough of the latter to explain it coherently or judge it fairly. My interest, however, lies in what Buddhists call the Way of Wisdom (*prajna*) rather than the Way of Powers (*siddhi*), because the indefinite enlargement of our powers and techniques seems in the end to be the pursuit of a mirage. One who is immortal and who has control of everything that happens to him strikes me as self-condemned to eternal boredom, since he lives in a world without mystery or surprise.

[6] Creel (1), p. 19.

*TAO: The Watercourse Way*

# 1. The Chinese Written Language

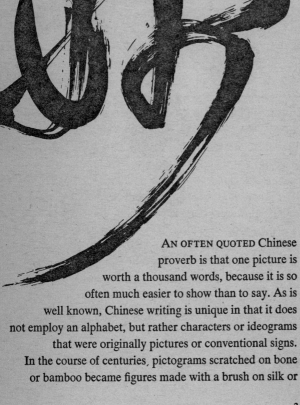

AN OFTEN QUOTED Chinese
proverb is that one picture is
worth a thousand words, because it is so
often much easier to show than to say. As is
well known, Chinese writing is unique in that it does
not employ an alphabet, but rather characters or ideograms
that were originally pictures or conventional signs.
In the course of centuries, pictograms scratched on bone
or bamboo became figures made with a brush on silk or

paper, few of which bear recognizable resemblance to their primitive forms or to what they are used to indicate, and they have grown immensely in number and in degree of abstraction.

Most Westerners—indeed most alphabetic people—and even some Chinese have the impression that this form of writing is impossibly complex and inefficient. In recent years there has been much talk of "rationalizing" Chinese by introducing an alphabet similar, perhaps, to the Japanese *hiragana* and *katakana*.[1] But this, I believe, would be a disaster.

We may not be aware of the extent to which alphabetic people are now using ideograms. International airports and highways abound with them because their meaning is at once obvious whatever one's native tongue may be. Table 1 is a partial list of such symbols, and Table 2 suggests how they might be employed in constructing sentences. Give rein to the imagination, and it becomes obvious that a rich visual language could be developed from these images which, with little difficulty, would be understandable to almost everyone without the necessity of learning a new spoken tongue. One would pronounce it in one's own. But it would take a long time for this language to develop a literature, and grow to the point where it could express subtle nuances of thought and feeling. However, computers would master it easily, and, as demonstrated in Table 2, such ideograms could convey complex relationships or configurations (*Gestalten*) much more rapidly than long, strung-out alphabetic sentences. For the ideogram gives one more information at a single glance, and in less space, than is given by the linear, alphabetic form

[1] These are highly simplified characters, the first cursive and the second scriptlike, used to designate the syllables of spoken Japanese. Written Japanese combines these alphabets with Chinese ideograms (*kanji*) so that, among other things, verbs may be conjugated and nouns declined. But I think it would be agreed that most Westerners find it far more difficult to read Japanese than Chinese. You must speak Japanese before you can read it.

# Table 1. A SELECTION OF WESTERN IDEOGRAMS

Astronomical, astrological, and meteorological:

Mathematical and electronic:

Directional, cartographic, and cautionary:

Chemical (archaic):

Religious and political:

Miscellaneous (though obvious in meaning):

Table 2. WESTERN IDEOGRAMS USED AS LANGUAGE

This simple tale hardly needs translation:

Sample compounds:

| | | | |
|---|---|---|---|
| ♂ Patriarchy | ♀ Matriarchy | ⚥ Sex equality | ⚨ Unisex |
| Joy in life | Fear of death | Eternal love | Crusade |
| Peaceful people | Mixed up | Fertile | Air pilot |
| Clear day, southwest wind | | Heavy rain, west wind, flood danger | |

of writing, which must also be pronounced to be understandable. Might there not be some connection between the length of time which it now takes to "complete" an education and the sheer mileage of print which one's eyes must scan?

For the natural universe is not a linear system. It involves an infinitude of variables interacting simultaneously, so that it would take incalculable aeons to translate even one moment of its operation into linear, alphabetic language. Let alone the universe! Take the planet Earth alone, or even what goes on

6

in a small pond or, for that matter, in the structure of the atom. This is where problems of language relate to Taoist philosophy, for the *Lao-tzu* book begins by saying that the Tao which can be spoken is not the eternal (or regular) Tao. Yet it goes on to show that there is some other way of understanding and getting along with the process of nature than by translating it into words. After all, the brain, the very organ of intelligence, defies linguistic description by even the greatest neurologists. It is thus that an ideographic language is a little closer to nature than one which is strictly linear and alphabetic. At any moment, nature is a simultaneity of patterns. An ideographic language is a *series* of patterns and, to that extent, still linear—but not so laboriously linear as an alphabetic language.

This critical point—that our organisms have ways of intelligent understanding beyond words and conscious attention, ways that can handle an unknown number of variables at the same time—will be discussed later. Suffice it to say now that the organization and regulation of thousands of bodily processes through the nervous system would be utterly beyond the capacity of deliberate thinking and planning—not to mention the relationships of those processes to the "external" world.

Now, as I have said, it would take years and years for a new and artificial ideographic language to develop a literature. But why go to the trouble when we already have Chinese? It is read by 800,000,000 people who pronounce it in at least seven different ways, or dialects, not including Japanese, which differ from each other far more radically than the King's English from Cockney or from the jazz argot of New Orleans. Furthermore, it has retained substantially the same form for at least 2,500 years, so that anyone speaking English today has far more difficulty in understanding Chaucer than a modern Chinese in making sense of Confucius. To some extent English—an incredibly complex and idiomatic language—has become the main international tongue, although Spanish would have been simpler. Isn't it possible that a second world language, in the written form, might be Chinese?

This is by no means so preposterous as most people would imagine, for our customary bafflement by Chinese ideograms is really a matter of uninformed prejudice. They are supposed to be outlandish, weird, devious, and as tricky as "the mysterious East." Although the K'ang-hsi dictionary of +1716 lists about 40,000 ideograms, a reasonably literate person needs about 5,000, and a comparably literate Westerner would know quite that many words of his own language. The difficulty of recognizing and identifying ideograms is surely no greater than with such other complex patterns as the various kinds of flowers, plants, butterflies, trees, and wild animals.

In other words, Chinese is simpler than it looks, and may, in general, be both written and read more rapidly than English. The English MAN requires ten strokes of the pen, whereas the Chinese *jen* 人 requires but two. TREE needs thirteen, but *mu* 木 is only four. WATER is sixteen, but *shui* 水 is five. MOUNTAIN is eighteen, but *shan* 山 is three. Even when we get really complicated, CONTEMPLATION is twenty-eight, whereas *kuan* 觀 is twenty-five. Roman capitals are the proper equivalents of these ideograms as shown, and though our longhand speeds things up it is nothing to its Chinese equivalent. Compare *nothing* with *wu* 无 . To contrast our writing with Chinese as to relative complexity, simply turn this page through a ninety-degree angle—and *then* look at English!

To simplify matters further, Chinese makes no rigid distinctions between parts of speech. Nouns and verbs are often interchangeable, and may also do duty as adjectives and ad-

## Table 3. THE EVOLUTION OF CHINESE WRITING

FIRST COLUMN: Archaic Script. SECOND: Small Seal style.
THIRD: Classical and Modern, based on use of the brush.

| | | | |
|---|---|---|---|
| ☉ | | 日 | Sun |
| | | 月 | Moon |
| | | 人 | Man, human being |
| | | 羊 | Sheep |
| | | 山 | Mountain |
| | | 入 | Enter (arrowhead) |
| | | 中 | Middle (ship's mast, with pennants above and below the bushell) |
| | | 至 | Arrive at (arrow hitting target) |
| | | 春 | Spring (wobbly plants still needing support of a cane) |
| | | 雨 | Rain |
| | | 行 | Move (crossroads) |
| | | 易 | Change (chameleon or lizard) |
| | | 元 | Origin, first (human profile with emphasis on head) |
| | | 生 | Birth, coming to be (growing plant) |
| | | 少 | Small (four grains) |
| | | 男 | Male (plow and field) |
| | | 土 | Earth (phallic totem) |
| | | 德 | Virtue, power, *mana* (abbreviation of the crossroad sign, "to move," plus the eye and heart, or "seeing" and "thinking-feeling") |

verbs. When serving as nouns they do not require the ritual nuisance of gender, wherewith adjectives must agree, nor are they declined, and when used as verbs they are not conjugated. When necessary, certain single ideograms are used to show whether the situation is past, present, or future. There is no pother over *is*, *was*, *were*, and *will be*, much less over *suis*, *es*, *est*, *sommes*, *êtes*, *sont*, *fus*, *fûmes*, *serais*, and *sois* as forms of the verb *être*, "to be." When translated very literally into English, Chinese reads much like a telegram:

上德不德是以不有德

Superior virtue not virtue is its being virtue.

This we must elaborate as, "Superior virtue is not intentionally virtuous, and this is just why it is virtue," but the Chinese is more shocking and "gives one to think."

From this it might seem that it is hard to be precise in Chinese, or to those clear distinctions which are necessary for scientific analysis. On the one hand, however, Chinese has the peculiar advantage of being able to say many things at once and to mean all of them, which is why there have been at least seventy English translations of Lao-tzu. On the other, Chinese uses compound words for precision. Thus *sheng* 生 which means, among other things, "to be born," can be specified as 生產 parturition, 生(出)世 to be born from the world, 生下 or 生義養 begotten, the latter having also the sense of bringing up; and then one distinguishes 胎生 birth from a womb, 卵生 birth from an egg, and 化生 birth by transformation, as with the butterfly.

An important part of Chinese grammar is the order of words. Although this is in many ways close to English, and does not, for example, remove verbs to the end of the sentence as in Latin and German, one must take care to distinguish 手背 the back of the hand(s) from 背手 hand(s) behind the back, and whereas 皇上 is the Emperor, 上皇 is his father, or the late Emperor. This is not so different in principle from ⟶↑ turn right and then go up, and ↑⟶ go up and turn right.

I have long been advocating the teaching of Chinese in secondary schools, not only because we must inevitably learn how to communicate with the Chinese themselves, but because, of all the high cultures, theirs is most different from ours in its ways of thinking. Every culture is based on assumptions so taken for granted that they are barely conscious, and it is only when we study highly different cultures and languages that we become aware of them. Standard average European (SAE) languages, for example, have sentences so structured that the verb (event) must be set in motion by the noun (thing)—thereby posing a metaphysical problem as tricky, and probably as meaningless, as that of the relation of mind to body. We cannot talk of "knowing" without assuming that there is some "who" or "what" that knows, not realizing that this is nothing more than a grammatical convention. The supposition that knowing requires a knower is based on a linguistic and not an existential rule, as becomes obvious when we consider that raining needs no rainer and clouding no clouder. Thus when a Chinese receives a formal invitation, he may reply simply with the word "Know," indicating that he is aware of the event and may or may not come.[2]

知

Consider, further, the astonishing experiment of Rozin, Poritsky, and Sotsky of the University of Pennsylvania, who discovered that second-grade children who were backward in reading could easily be taught to read Chinese, and could construct simple sentences within four weeks.[3] I do not know

[2] Lin Yutang (1), p. 164.
[3] Rozin, Poritsky, and Sotsky (1), pp. 1264–67.

if anyone has yet studied this method with deaf children, but it seems obvious that an ideographic language would be their ideal means of written communication. One notices often that both Chinese and Japanese people in conversation will draw ideograms in the air or on the table with their fingers to clarify ambiguity or vagueness in the spoken word. (It is quite a trick to draw them backwards or upside down for the benefit of the person facing you!)

永

It is sometimes said that Chinese writing (as well as painting) comprises an "alphabet" in the sense that it has a finite number of standard components.[4] It is said, not quite correctly, that the ideogram *yung,* "eternal," contains all the basic strokes used in Chinese writing, though I cannot see that it includes the fundamental "bone stroke" � or such formations as ╰乙厶 . As soon as one is familiar with the elemental strokes and component forms of the ideograms, they are more easily recognized and remembered, even before one knows their English meaning. Reading Chinese is fundamentally what communications technicians call "pattern recognition"—a function of the mind which is, as yet, only rudimentarily mastered by the computer, because it is a nonlinear function. The mind recognizes instantly that A ɑ *A a* A a as well as 𝒜𝓡𝒜𝒜𝕬 are all the same letter, but as of today (1973) the computer has trouble with this. But it does not seem at all inconceivable that a computer could absorb the *k'ai-shu,* which is the formal and rigid style

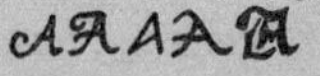

楷書

4 Aside from the basic strokes (of the brush), there are slightly more complex components, roughly equivalent to the simpler forms of the 214 "radicals" whereby the ideograms are classified in dictionaries. It seems to me that by far the most convenient and sensibly arranged beginner's dictionary is Arthur Rose-Innes (1), even though the pronunciations given are Japanese. As to the use of a similar principle in painting, see Mai-mai Sze (1), vol. 2, the section entitled "The Mustard-Seed Garden." Also Chiang Yee (1), *Chinese Calligraphy*.

of Chinese printing, and so begin to approach a nonlinear method of thinking.

The idea of nonlinearity is unfamiliar to many people, so I should perhaps explain it in more detail. A good organist, using ten fingers and two feet, could—by playing chords— keep twelve melodies going at once, though, unless he was very dexterous with his feet, they would have to be of the same rhythm. But he could certainly render a six-part fugue— four with the hands and two with the feet—and in mathematical and scientific language each of these parts would be called a variable. The performance of each organ of the body is also a variable—as is also, in this context, the temperature, the constitution of the atmosphere, the bacterial environment, the wavelength of various forms of radiation, and the gravitational field. But we have no idea of how many variables could be distinguished in any given natural situation. A variable is a process (e.g., melody, pulse, vibration) which can be isolated, identified, and measured by conscious attention.

The problem of coping with variables is twofold. First: how do we recognize and identify *a* variable, or *a* process? For example, can we think of the heart as separate from the veins, or the branches from the tree? Just what exact delineations distinguish the bee process from the flower process? These distinctions are always somewhat arbitrary and conventional, even when described with very exact language, for the distinctions reside more in the language than in what it describes. Second: there is no known limit to the number of variables that may be involved in any natural, or physical, event—such as the hatching of an egg. The boundary of the shell is hard and clear, but when we begin to think about it, it washes into considerations of molecular biology, climate, nuclear physics, techniques of poultry farming, ornithological sexology, and so on and so on until we realize that this "single event" should—if we could manage it—be considered in relation to the whole universe. But conscious attention, relying on the instruments of spelled-out words in lines, or numbers in lines, cannot keep simultaneous track of more than a few of the variables which are isolated and described by these instruments. From the standpoint of linear description, there is just much too much going on at each moment. We persuade ourselves, then, that we are attending to some really important or significant things, much as a newspaper editor will select "the news" out of an infinitude of happenings.

The ear cannot detect as many variables at the same time as the eye, for sound is a slower vibration than light. Alphabetic writing is a representation of sound, whereas the ideogram represents vision and, furthermore, represents the world directly—not being a sign for a sound which is the name of a thing. As for names, the sound "bird" has nothing in it that reminds one of a bird, and for some reason it would strike us as childish to substitute more direct names, such as tweetie, powee, or quark.

Aside from all these utilitarian advantages of the ideogram, there is also its formal beauty. This is not simply because, to our eyes, it is exotic and unintelligible. No one appreciates the beauty of this writing more than the Chinese and Japanese themselves, though one might suppose that their familiarity with it would have made them indifferent to anything but its meaning. On the contrary: the practice of calligraphy is considered in the Far East as a fine art, along with painting and sculpture. A written scroll, hanging in one's alcove, is by no means to be compared to some biblical admonition, printed in Gothic letters, framed, and hung on the wall. The importance of the latter is its message, whereas the importance of the former is its visual beauty and its expression of the character of the writer.

I have practiced Chinese calligraphy for many years, and am not yet a master of the art, which could be described as dancing with brush and ink on absorbent paper. Because ink is mostly water, Chinese calligraphy—controlling the flow of water with the soft brush as distinct from the hard pen— requires that you go with the flow. If you hesitate, hold the brush too long in one place, or hurry, or try to correct what you have written, the blemishes are all too obvious. But if you write well there is at the same time the sensation that the work is happening on its own, that the brush is writing all by itself —as a river, by following the line of least resistance, makes elegant curves. The beauty of Chinese calligraphy is thus the same beauty which we recognize in moving water, in foam, spray, eddies, and waves, as well as in clouds, flames, and weavings of smoke in sunlight. The Chinese call this kind of beauty the following of *li,* an ideogram which referred origi-  nally to the grain in jade and wood, and which Needham translates as "organic pattern," although it is more generally understood as the "reason" or "principle" of things. *Li* is the pattern of behavior which comes about when one is in accord with the Tao, the watercourse of nature. The patterns of moving air are of the same character, and so the Chinese idea of elegance is expressed as *feng-liu,* the flowing of wind.

Now this going with the wind or the current, plus the intel- ligence pattern of the human organism, is the whole art of sailing—of keeping wind in your sails while tacking in a con- trary direction. Buckminster Fuller has suggested that sailors were the first great technologists, studying the stars for naviga- tion, realizing that Earth is a globe, inventing block-and- tackle devices for hoisting sails (and thus cranes), and understanding the rudiments of meteorology. Likewise Thor Heyer-dahl (1) in his Kon-Tiki expedition reconstructed the most primitive sailing raft to see where the winds and currents of the Pacific would take him from Peru, and was amazed to discover how his act of faith was honored by nature's co-operation. Along the same line of thought: just as it is more intelligent to sail than to row, our technology is surely better advised to use the tides, the rivers, and the sun for energy rather than fossil fuels and the capricious power of nuclear fission.

Just as Chinese writing is at least one step closer to nature than ours, so the ancient philosophy of the Tao is of a skill-ful and intelligent following of the course, current, and grain of natural phenomena—seeing human life as an integral feature of the world process, and not as something alien and opposed to it. Looking at this philosophy with the needs and problems of modern civilization in mind, it suggests an attitude to the world which must underlie all our efforts towards an eco-logical technology. For the development of such a technology is not just a matter of the techniques themselves, but of the psychological attitude of the technician.

Hitherto, Western science has stressed the attitude of objec-tivity—a cold, calculating, and detached attitude through which it appears that natural phenomena, including the human organism, are nothing but mechanisms. But, as the word itself implies, a universe of mere objects is objectionable. We feel justified in exploiting it ruthlessly, but now we are belatedly realizing that the ill-treatment of the environment is damage to ourselves—for the simple reason that subject and object cannot be separated, and that we and our surroundings are the process of a unified field, which is what the Chinese call Tao. In the long run, we simply have no other alternative than to work along with this process by attitudes and methods which could be as effective technically as *judo*, the "gentle Tao," is effective athletically. As human beings have to make the gamble of trusting one another in order to have any kind of workable community, we must also take the risk of trimming our sails to the winds of nature. For our "selves" are inseparable from this kind of universe, and there is nowhere else to be.

# 2. The Yin-Yang Polarity

AT THE VERY ROOTS
of Chinese thinking and feeling
there lies the principle of polarity.
which is not to be confused with the ideas of opposition
or conflict. In the metaphors of other cultures,
light is at war with darkness, life with death, good
with evil, and the positive with the negative, and thus an

idealism to cultivate the former and be rid of the latter flourishes throughout much of the world. To the traditional way of Chinese thinking, this is as incomprehensible as an electric current without both positive and negative poles, for polarity is the principle that + and —, north and south, are different aspects of one and the same system, and that the disappearance of either one of them would be the disappearance of the system.

People who have been brought up in the aura of Christian and Hebrew aspirations find this frustrating, because it seems to deny any possibility of progress, an ideal which flows from their linear (as distinct from cyclic) view of time and history. Indeed, the whole enterprise of Western technology is "to make the world a better place"—to have pleasure without pain, wealth without poverty, and health without sickness. But, as is now becoming obvious, our violent efforts to achieve this ideal with such weapons as DDT, penicillin, nuclear energy, automotive transportation, computers, industrial farming, damming, and compelling everyone, by law, to be superficially "good and healthy" are creating more problems than they solve. We have been interfering with a complex system of relationships which we do not understand, and the more we study its details, the more it eludes us by revealing still more details to study. As we try to comprehend and control the world it runs away from us. Instead of chafing at this situation, a Taoist would ask what it means. What is that which always retreats when pursued? Answer: yourself. Idealists (in the moral sense of the word) regard the universe as different and separate from themselves—that is, as a system of external objects which needs to be subjugated. Taoists view the universe as the same as, or inseparable from, themselves—so that Lao-tzu could say, "Without leaving my house, I know the whole universe." [104*a*]¹ This implies that the art of life is more like navigation than warfare, for what is important is to understand the winds, the tides, the currents, the seasons, and the principles of growth and decay, so that one's actions may use them and not fight them. In this sense, the Taoist attitude is not opposed to technology per se. Indeed, the Chuang-tzu writings are full of references to crafts and skills perfected by this very principle of "going with the grain." The point is therefore that technology is destructive only in the hands of people who do not realize that they are one and the same process as the universe. Our overspecialization in conscious attention and linear thinking has led to neglect, or ignore-ance, of the basic principles and rhythms of this process, of which the foremost is polarity.

In Chinese the two poles of cosmic energy are *yang* (positive) and *yin* (negative), and their conventional signs are respectively —— and — — . The ideograms indicate the sunny and shady sides of a hill, *fou*, and they are associated with the masculine and the feminine, the firm and the yielding, the strong and the weak, the light and the dark, the rising and the falling, heaven and earth, and they are even recognized in such everyday matters as cooking as the spicy and the bland. Thus the art of life is not seen as holding to *yang* and banishing *yin*, but as keeping the two in balance, because there cannot be one without the other. When regarding them as the masculine and the feminine, the reference is not so much to male and female individuals as to characteristics which are dominant in, but not confined to, each of the two sexes. Ob-

陽 陰
阜 or 阝

---

¹ *Lao-tzu* 47, tr. auct. The number in brackets refers to the page on which this quotation is reproduced in Chinese calligraphy. The letter *a* identifies this quotation on that page. A note on p. 105 below explains the arrangement of the calligraphy, which appears on pp. 56–73 and 99–104.

viously, the male has the convex penis and the female the concave vagina; and though people have regarded the former as a possession and the latter as a deprivation (Freud's "penis envy"), any fool should be able to recognize that one cannot have the outstanding without the instanding, and that a rampant *membrum virile* is no good without somewhere to put it, and vice versa.* But the male individual must not neglect his female component, nor the female her male. Thus Lao-tzu says:

> Knowing the male but keeping the female, one becomes a universal stream. Becoming a universal stream, one is not separated from eternal virtue.[2] [104*b*]

The *yang* and the *yin* are principles, not men and women, so that there can be no true relationship between the affectedly tough male and the affectedly flimsy female.

The key to the relationship between *yang* and *yin* is called 相生 *hsiang sheng,* mutual arising or inseparability. As Lao-tzu puts it:

> When everyone knows beauty as beautiful, there is already ugliness;

---

* Besides, the female also has a convex sexual part—the clitoris—smaller but possibly more potent in pleasure than that of the male (more, and more sustained, orgasms). She also has a convex breast, compared with the male's flat chest. She is endowed, above all, with the equipment to bear children—envied by many men nowadays—and her beauty is more subtle than the peacocklike opulence outstanding in the male of the species. Chinese men have always known this "balance in imbalance." Perhaps this is one of the reasons for the universal suppression of the woman by her man.

The asterisk indicates additional notes made by Al Chung-liang Huang, who believes these changes and extensions would have been made by Alan Watts himself had he lived and continued to improve upon the existing manuscript. All comments are based on discussions between Al Huang and Alan Watts during the course of their collaboration in writing this book. Some are adapted or taken directly from the words of friends who read Alan's first draft and were kind enough to return comments.

[2] *Lao-tzu* 28, tr. auct.

When everyone knows good as goodness, there is already
    evil.
"To be" and "not to be" arise mutually;
Difficult and easy are mutually realized;
Long and short are mutually contrasted;
High and low are mutually posited; . . .
Before and after are in mutual sequence.[3] [104*c*]

They are thus like the different, but inseparable, sides of a
coin, the poles of a magnet, or pulse and interval in any
vibration. There is never the ultimate possibility that either
one will win over the other, for they are more like lovers
wrestling than enemies fighting.[4] But it is difficult in our logic
to see that being and nonbeing are mutually generative and
mutually supportive, for it is the great and imaginary terror
of Western man that nothingness will be the permanent
end of the universe. We do not easily grasp the point that the
void is creative, and that being comes from nonbeing as sound
from silence and light from space.

    Thirty spokes unite at the wheel's hub;
    It is the center hole [literally, "from their not being"]
        that makes it useful.
    Shape clay into a vessel;
    It is the space within that makes it useful.
    Cut out doors and windows for a room;
    It is the holes which make it useful.
    Therefore profit comes from what is there;
    Usefulness from what is not there.[5] [104*d*]

I do not know if this point can really be argued in our logic,
but I find it impossible to conceive any form whatsoever without the component of relatively empty space. We ignore space

[3] *Lao-tzu* 2, tr. auct.

[4] It is thus of interest that a common Chinese expression for sexual
intercourse is *hua chen*, the flowery combat, in which, of course, there is
no wish in either partner to annihilate the other.

[5] *Lao-tzu* 11, tr. Gia-fu Feng (1), n.p., mod. auct.

just because it is uniform, as water to fish and air to birds. It is almost impossible to give intelligible descriptions of elements or dimensions which are constant in all experiences—such as consciousness, time, motion, or electricity. Yet electricity is very much here, having measurable and controllable properties. But Professor Harold A. Wilson, writing on "Electricity" in the 1947 *Encyclopaedia Britannica,* says:

> The study of electricity to-day comprehends a vast range of phenomena, in all of which we are brought back ultimately to the fundamental conceptions of electric charge and of electric and magnetic fields. *These conceptions are at present ultimates,* not explained in terms of others. In the past there have been various attempts to explain them in terms of electric fluids and aethers having the properties of material bodies known to us by the study of mechanics. To-day, however, we find that the phenomena of electricity cannot be so explained, and the tendency is *to explain all other phenomena in terms of electricity, taken as a fundamental thing.* The question, "What is electricity?" is therefore essentially unanswerable, if by it is sought an explanation of the nature of electricity in terms of material bodies.[6]

That, from a scientist, is pure metaphysics. Change a few words, and it would be Saint Thomas Aquinas writing about God.

 Yet, as I feel it intuitively, "space" and "void" (*k'ung*) are very much here, and every child teases itself out of thought by trying to imagine space expanding out and out with no limit. This space is not "just nothing" as we commonly use that expression, for I cannot get away from the sense that space and my awareness of the universe are the same, and call to mind

---

[6] *EB* (1947), vol. 8, p. 182. Italics mine. This is reminiscent of Lao-tzu beginning, "The Tao which can be explained is not the eternal Tao," and then going on to write a whole book about it; for the article which follows this paragraph is a vastly learned discussion of the properties and behavior of this unknown "ultimate."

the words of the Ch'an (Zen) Patriarch Hui-neng, writing
eleven centuries after Lao-tzu:

> The capacity of mind is broad and huge, like the vast sky.
> Do not sit with a mind fixed on emptiness. If you do you will
> fall into a neutral kind of emptiness. Emptiness includes the
> sun, moon, stars, and planets, the great earth, mountains and
> rivers, all trees and grasses, bad men and good men, bad
> things and good things, heaven and hell; they are all in the
> midst of emptiness. The emptiness of human nature is also
> like this.[7]

Thus the *yin-yang* principle is that the somethings and the
nothings, the ons and the offs, the solids and the spaces, as
well as the wakings and the sleepings and the alternations of
existing and not existing, are mutually necessary. How, one
might ask, would you know that you are alive unless you had
once been dead? How can one speak of reality or is-ness
except in the context of the polar apprehension of void?

*Yang* and *yin* are in some ways parallel to the (later)
Buddhist view of form, *se,* and emptiness, *k'ung*—of which
the *Hridaya Sutra* says, "That which is form is just that which
is emptiness, and that which is emptiness is just that which is
form." This seeming paradox is at once intelligible in terms
of the idea of clarity, *ch'ing,* for we think of clarity at once
as translucent and unobstructed space, and as form articulate
in every detail—as what photographers, using finely polished
lenses, call "high resolution"—and this takes us back to what
Lao-tzu said of the usefulness of doors and windows. Through
perfect nothing we see perfect something. In much the same
way, philosophers of the Yin-Yang School (−3rd century)
saw the positive —— and negative —— as aspects of *t'ai
chi,* the Great Ultimate, initially represented as an empty
circle, as *wu chi,* although *chi* seems to have had the original

[7] *Tan-ching* 24, tr. Yampolsky (1), p. 146.

meaning of a ridgepole upon which, of course, the two sides of a roof, *yang* and *yin*, would lean.

The *yin-yang* principle is not, therefore, what we would ordinarily call a dualism, but rather an explicit duality expressing an implicit unity. The two principles are, as I have suggested, not opposed like the Zoroastrian Ahura Mazda and Ahriman, but in love, and it is curious that their traditional emblem is that double helix which is at once the pattern of sexual communication and of the spiral galaxies.

> One *yin* and one *yang* is called the Tao. The passionate union of *yin* and *yang* and the copulation of husband and wife is the eternal pattern of the universe. If heaven and earth did not mingle, whence would everything receive life?[8]

The practical problem of life was not to let their wrestling match get out of hand. Only recently have the Chinese set their hearts upon some kind of utopia, but this must be understood as the necessary reaction to years and years of foreign exploitation, anarchy, and extreme poverty.* But in the −4th century Chuang-tzu wrote:

> Thus, those who say that they would have right without its correlate, wrong, or good government without its correlate, misrule, do not apprehend the great principles of the universe, nor the nature of all creation. One might as well talk of the existence of Heaven without that of Earth, or of the negative principle without the positive, which is clearly impossible. Yet people keep on discussing it without stop; such people must be either fools or knaves.[9] [58*a*]

[8] *Ch'eng-tzu,* tr. Forke (1), p. 68, mod. auct. See also the works of Ch'eng Ming-tao and Ch'eng Yi-ch'uan in Graham (1).

* And looking back into Chinese history, there has been one revolution after another, each swinging with equal urgency to the opposite extreme from the previous government. Cyclically, after an equilibrium has been attained, a new imbalance begins to rise to its height, then a new revolution becomes necessary. Most Chinese view the present Chinese government as one phase of the moon. The name of the king or ruler may change from time to time, but the Chinese people, the human being and his nature, will remain constant.

[9] *Chuang-tzu* 17, tr. Lin Yutang (3), p. 51.

易經
兩儀

Both Lao-tzu (once, in ch. 42) and Chuang-tzu (many times) mention the *yin-yang* polarity, but there is no reference to the *I Ching,* or *Book of Changes,* in which the permutations and combinations of the two forces (*liang yi*) are worked out in detail, in terms of the sixty-four hexagrams of *yin* and *yang* lines. Yet the *I Ching* is supposed to have been the most ancient of all the Chinese classics, dating from as far back as the —2nd or even —3rd millennium, and thus to exhibit the basic patterns of Chinese thought and culture. But in that neither Lao-tzu nor Chuang-tzu mentions it, quotes it, nor uses its characteristic terminology, the hoary antiquity and authority of this text must be called in question.[10] On the other hand, since at least the —3rd century Chinese savants have commented on this work in such a way as to perfume it with their thoughts and thus to give it a philosophical profundity. Readers of the great Wilhelm translation, and especially those who use it for divination, should be aware that he has interspersed the earliest forms of the text with passages from the "Wings," or Appendices, most of which are certainly later than —250. In other words, the Wilhelm translation gives us a true picture of the *I Ching* as used and understood in China in relatively modern times. But my guess is that in the —5th and —4th centuries it was circulating as an orally transmitted folk wisdom, of indeterminable antiquity, comparable to the art of reading tea-leaves or the lines on the palm of the hand. There might have been written versions of it, but they would have been of the status of the *Farmer's Almanac* or popular guides to the meaning of dreams.

Thus the *I Ching,* as a specific text, does not appear to have influenced Taoism until after the days of Lao-tzu and Chuang-tzu. Nevertheless, there is a common element in the rationale

---

[10] The reference to Confucius' reverence for the book in the *Lun Yü* is of very doubtful veracity, for there is no reference to it in the Lu version of the *Analects.* See Waley (1), p. 124 *n.*

of the *I Ching* and early Taoist philosophy. Briefly, this element is the recognition that opposites are polar, or interdependent, and that there is something in us—which Groddeck, Freud, and Jung called "the Unconscious"—which may be called upon for a higher wisdom than can be figured out by logic. In more up-to-date terms one might say that the labyrinth of the nervous system can integrate more variables than the scanning process of conscious attention, though this way of putting it is still a concession to the mechanistic assumptions of +19th-century science. But one uses such language mainly to stay in communication with colleagues who have not outgrown it.

The *I Ching* involves a method for the random sorting of milfoil twigs or coins. The twigs or the coins are thus sorted or thrown six times, with a question seriously held in mind. Each casting results in a *yin* — — or *yang* ——— line, so that one builds up, from the bottom, a hexagram such as:

The hexagram is composed of two trigrams—in this case, the upper signifies fire and the lower water—and is the last of the sixty-four hexagrams. Turning to the text, one reads:

### THE JUDGMENT
Before completion.   Success.
But if the little fox, after nearly completing
    the crossing,
Gets his tail in the water,
There is nothing that would further.

### *THE IMAGE*

Fire over water:
The image of the condition before transition.
Thus the superior man is careful
In the differentiation of things,
So that each finds its place.[11]

The comment is invariably oracular, vague, and ambivalent, but a person taking it seriously will use it like a Rorschach blot and project into it, from his "unconscious," whatever there is in him to find in it. This is surely a way of allowing oneself to think without keeping a tight guard on one's thoughts, whether logical or moral. The same sort of process is at work in the psychoanalytic interpretation of dreams and in eidetic vision, whereby we descry faces, forms, and pictures in the grain of wood or marble, or in the shapes of clouds. In this connection I must quote some anecdotes about Ch'an (Zen) painters of the +13th century.

About the year 1215, a Zen priest called Mü Ch'i came to Hangchow, where he rebuilt a ruined monastery. By rapid swirls of ink he attempted, with undeniable success, to capture the moments of exaltation and set down the fleeting visions which he obtained from the frenzy of wine, the stupor of tea, or the vacancy of inanition. Ch'en Jung, about the same time, was noted for the simplicity of his life and the competence with which he fulfilled his duties as a magistrate. . . . Finally, he was admired for his habits of a confirmed drunkard. "He made clouds by splashing ink on his pictures. For mists he spat out water. When wrought up by wine he uttered a great shout and, seizing his hat, used it as a brush, roughly smearing his drawing; after which he finished his work with a proper brush." One of the first painters of the sect, Wang Hsia, who lived in the early ninth century, would perform when he was drunk real *tours de force,* going so far as to plunge his head into a bucket of ink

11 Wilhelm (1), p. 249.

and flop it over a piece of silk on which there appeared, as if by magic, lakes, trees, enchanted mountains. But none seems to have carried emancipation further, among these priests, than Ying Yü-chien, secretary of the famous temple Ching-tzü ssii, who would take a cat-like pleasure in spattering and lacerating the sheet.[12]

The remarks about Ch'en Jung, in particular, suggest that these gentlemen, having spattered the silk with ink, would contemplate the mess until they could project the shapes and outlines of landscape. Thereafter they would take "the proper brush" and with a few touches bring it out for all to see.

Cases of this use of the creative un-, sub-, or superconscious are so numerous among painters (including Leonardo), physicists, mathematicians, writers, and musicians that we need not go into further examples. I am sure that the *I Ching* oracles are used in the same way as these painters used splashes of ink—as forms to be contemplated empty-mindedly until the hidden meaning reveals itself, in accordance with one's own unconscious tendencies.[13] As with astrology, the rituals and calculations of consulting the *I Ching* are a kind of doodling which quiets the repressive anxieties of consciousness and, with luck, allows useful insights to emerge from one's deeper centers.*

The book, therefore, is not entirely superstitious. Consider that when we are about to make decisions we usually collect

---

[12] Duthuit (1), pp. 33–34.

[13] Some accounts say that the *I Ching* hexagrams were derived from contemplating the cracks which appeared when the shell of a tortoise was heated, and this would certainly support the idea that its method was based on something like eidetic vision.

* Hokusai (1760–1829), one of the great Ukiyoye masters of Japan, was once summoned by the Emperor to paint at court. He first dipped the feet of a chicken in blue ink and gently dragged them over a long scroll of rice paper. Then he dipped another chicken's feet in vermilion ink and simply let the chicken walk freely upon the scroll. After this was done, he bowed deeply to his royal patron and showed him the painting "Autumn Leaves Falling on the Yangtze River."

as much information as we can; but often it is so ambivalent that we are reduced to tossing a coin which can say either "Yes" or "No," "Do" or "Don't." Would there be some advantage to having, as it were, a coin with sixty-four sides? The hexagram drawn above might be saying, "No, yes, no; yes, no, yes." Also it should be noted as a curious characteristic of the *I Ching* that there are no absolutely good or bad hexagrams in its cyclic series.*

This may be illustrated by the Taoist story of a farmer whose horse ran away. That evening the neighbors gathered to commiserate with him since this was such bad luck. He said, "May be." The next day the horse returned, but brought with it six wild horses, and the neighbors came exclaiming at his good fortune. He said, "May be." And then, the following day, his son tried to saddle and ride one of the wild horses, was thrown, and broke his leg. Again the neighbors came to offer their sympathy for the misfortune. He said, "May be." The day after that, conscription officers came to the village to seize young men for the army, but because of the broken leg the farmer's son was rejected. When the neighbors came in to say how fortunately everything had turned out, he said, "May be."[14]

The *yin-yang* view of the world is serenely cyclic. Fortune and misfortune, life and death, whether on small scale or vast, come and go everlastingly without beginning or end, and the whole system is protected from monotony by the fact that, in just the same way, remembering alternates with forgetting. This is the Good of good-and-bad. Hasegawa Saburo, the Japanese artist, told me that when he was in Peking with the

---

* For other useful observations on the *I Ching*, as a departure from the basic texts, read R. G. H. Siu, *The Man of Many Qualities*, and Khigh Alx Dhiegh, *The Eleventh Wing*.

[14] Popular folktale, *Huai Nan Tzu* 18, p. 6a. A version of this story, as told by Lieh-tzu, appears in Lin Yutang (1), p. 160.

Japanese invaders in 1936 he would watch the eyes of the Chinese crowds—the resigned, cynical, and faintly amused expression which seemed to say, "We've seen the likes of you many times before, and you too will go away." And he imitated the expression with his own face.

If there is anything basic to Chinese culture, it is an attitude of respectful trust towards nature and human nature—despite wars, revolutions, mass executions, starvation, floods, droughts, and all manner of horrors. There is nothing in their philosophy like the notion of original sin or the Theravada Buddhist feeling that existence itself is a disaster.[15] Chinese philosophy, whether Taoist or Confucian or, one hopes, even Maoist, takes it as a basic premise that if you cannot trust nature and other people, you cannot trust yourself. If you cannot trust yourself, you cannot even trust your mistrust of yourself—so that without this underlying trust in the whole system of nature you are simply paralyzed. So Lao-tzu makes the sage, as ruler, say:

> I take no action and people are reformed.
> I enjoy peace and people become honest.
> I use no force and people become rich.
> I have no ambitions and people return to the good and simple life.[16] [103a]

Ultimately, of course, it is not really a matter of oneself, on the one hand, trusting nature, on the other. It is a matter of realizing that oneself and nature are one and the same process, which is the Tao. True, this is an oversimplification, for one knows very well that some people cannot be trusted and that the unpredictable ways of nature are not always one's own preconceived way, so that basic faith in the system involves taking risks. But when no risk is taken there is no

15 A feeling which is, however, more theoretical than actual. The peoples of Lanka, Burma, and Thailand, where Theravada Buddhism prevails, are an unaccountably joyous and sociable folk.

16 Lao-tzu 57, tr. Gia-fu Feng (1), n.p., mod. auct.

freedom. It is thus that, in an industrial society, the plethora of laws made for our personal safety convert the land into a nursery, and policemen hired to protect us become self-serving busybodies.

Early Taoism presupposes the *yin-yang* principle but seems, in the main, to have rejected another view which went along with it, the theory of the five elements or energies (*wu hsing*), 五行 whose first celebrated exponent was Tsou Yen (c. −350 to −270), master of the Yin-Yang Chia, who came from the state of Ch'i in the northeast of China. He was, by all accounts, a man of immense erudition and imagination, consulted and honored by rulers, and one of the first serious geographers of China who pointed out, among other things, that China, so far from being the Middle Kingdom, occupied but one part in eighty-one of the earth's surface. The five energies were identified, or better, symbolized, as (1) *wood,* which as fuel gives rise to (2) *fire,* which creates ash and gives rise to (3) *earth,* which in its mines contains (4) *metal,* which (as on the surface of a metal mirror) attracts dew and so gives rise to (5) *water,* and this in turn nourishes (1) *wood.* This is called the *hsiang sheng,* or "mutually arising" 相生 order of the forces, and utterly fanciful as it may seem to us, it has the special interest of describing a cycle in which cause and effect are not sequential but simultaneous. The forces are so interdependent that no one can exist without all the others, just as there can be no *yang* without *yin.*

The forces were also arranged in the order of "mutual conquest" (*hsiang sheng,* but *sheng* is a different ideogram) in 相勝 which (1) *wood,* in the form of a plow, overcomes (2) *earth* which, by damming and constraint, conquers (3) *water* which, by quenching, overcomes (4) *fire* which, by melting, liquifies (5) *metal* which, in turn, cuts (1) *wood.* This reminds one of the children's game of paper, scissors, and stone, in which two players hold up their right hands at precisely the same moment. Held as fist, the hand represents stone; fingers in a V represent scissors; and the open palm represents paper. Stone blunts scissors, scissors cut paper, and paper wraps stone; so that if fist and palm are held up at the same time, palm is the winner, and so on.

In later times other such cycles were elaborated as, for example, the sequence (1) receiving breath, (2) being in the womb, (3) being nourished, (4) birth, (5) being bathed, (6) assuming cap and girdle, or puberty, (7) becoming an official, (8) flourishing, (9) weakening, (10) sickness, (11) death, and (12) burial.[17] This is curiously similar to the Buddhist Chain of Dependent Origination (*pratitya samutpada*) and may have been influenced by it, though in the latter the stages are (1) ignore-ance, (2) activity generating karma, (3) consciousness, (4) name-and-form, (5) sense organs, (6) contact, (7) feeling, (8) craving, (9) clinging, (10) becoming, (11) birth, (12) old age and death—which is again (1). *Samutpada* (much as some philologists may disapprove) can roughly be broken down as *sam-* (all together) *ut-* (out) *pada* (stepping), which is the same principle as the Chinese "mutually arising." Conscious attention scans the cycle sequentially, but existentially the whole clock is present while the hand moves. This is the sense of Lao-tzu's (ch. 2) "Before and after are in mutual sequence." There cannot be any "before" unless there is an "after," and vice versa, and six o'clock has no meaning without the whole series of hours from one through twelve.

> (From) Tao arises One; from One arises Two; from Two arises Three; and from Three arise the ten thousand things.[18]
> [103*b*]

In other words, no number has any significance except in

[17] Cf. Needham (1), vol. 2, p. 250. And for a full discussion of the *yin-yang* and *wu hsing* theories see ibid., sec. 13*c*., pp. 232 et seq.
[18] *Lao-tzu* 42, tr. auct.

五行

relation to those which precede and those which follow. Thus if we were to omit 13 from the series of integers (as they do in some apartment buildings), 1,000 would have to be understood ridiculously and inconveniently as 999, since that would be the actual value of the figure. The point is simply that you cannot omit one integer without upsetting the entire system. What we are beginning to get at here is a view of the universe which is organic and relational—not a mechanism, artifact, or creation, and by no means analogous to a political or military hierarchy in which there is a Supreme Commander.

In the *yin-yang* and *wu hsing* theories this organic view of the world is implicit, but it becomes explicit in Lao-tzu, and far more so in Chuang-tzu and Lieh-tzu, though one does not find it stressed in Confucian thought (absorbed as that was with political and social matters) until the Neo-Confucianism of Chu Hsi (+1131 to +1200), in which all the compatible threads of Confucianism, Taoism, and Buddhism are woven together. Perhaps the greatest exponent of this organic view was the Buddhist Fa-tsang (+643 to +712) of the Mahayanist Hua-yen School, whose image of the universe was a multidimensional network of jewels, each one containing the reflections of all the others *ad infinitum*. Each jewel was a *shih*, or "thing-event," and his principle of *shih shih wu ai* ("between one thing-event and another is no obstruction") expounded the mutual interpenetration and interdependence of everything happening in the universe. Pick up a blade of grass and all the worlds come with it. In other words, the whole cosmos is implicit in every member of it, and every point in it may be regarded as its center. This is the bare and basic principle of the organic view, to which we shall return in our discussion of the meaning of Tao.

事事無礙

In the meantime—and before we go any further—it should

be said that to a true Taoist even such a mildly academic discussion of the Tao as this would seem pretentious and unnecessary. I am, of course, puttering about in Chinese literature and philosophy as one who takes care of a kitchen garden as distinct from a big farm, and have the same sort of affection for the literary atmosphere of the Tao—the texts, the calligraphy, the paintings, and even the Chinese dictionaries—that one might have for a small row of tomatoes or runner beans, a plum tree, and a modest stand of corn.

However, a one-sidedly literary and academic approach to the Tao gives nothing of its essence, so that to understand what follows the reader must now, and at each subsequent reading, allow himself to be in a proper state of mind. You are asked—temporarily, of course—to lay aside all your philosophical, religious, and political opinions, and to become almost like an infant, knowing nothing. Nothing, that is, except what you actually hear, see, feel, and smell. Take it that you are not going anywhere but here, and that there never was, is, or will be any other time than now. Simply be aware of what actually *is* without giving it names and without judging it, for you are now feeling out reality itself instead of ideas and opinions *about* it. There is no point in trying to suppress the babble of words and ideas that goes on in most adult brains, so if it won't stop, let it go on as it will, and listen to it as if it were the sound of traffic or the clucking of hens.

Let your ears hear whatever they want to hear; let your eyes see whatever they want to see; let your mind think whatever it wants to think; let your lungs breathe in their own rhythm. Do not expect any special result, for in this wordless and idealess state, where can there be past or future, and where any notion of purpose? Stop, look, and listen . . . and stay there awhile before you go on reading.

# 3. Tao

"THE TAO is that from which
one cannot deviate; that from which
one can deviate is not the Tao."[1] [56a]
This sentence from the *Chung Yung,*
or "Doctrine of the Mean," suggests that there is no
analogy between Tao and the Western ideas of God
and of divine or natural law, which can be obeyed or
disobeyed. The saying is a hard one, because both Lao-tzu

[1] See footnote 3 below.

and Chuang-tzu speak of forced actions which are at variance with the Tao. The paradox is resolved in a dialogue which occurred centuries later between the Ch'an masters Nan-ch'üan and Chao-chou:

> Chao-Chou asked, "What is the Tao?"
> The master [Nan-ch'üan] replied, "Your ordinary consciousness is the Tao."
> "How can one return into accord with it?"
> "By intending to accord you immediately deviate."
> "But without intention, how can one know the Tao?"
> "The Tao," said the master, "belongs neither to knowing nor to not knowing. Knowing is false understanding; not knowing is blind ignorance. If you really understand the Tao beyond doubt, it's like the empty sky. Why drag in right and wrong?"[2] [56b]

In other words, people try to force issues only when not realizing that it can't be done—that there is no way of deviating from the watercourse of nature. You may imagine that you are outside, or separate from, the Tao and thus able to follow it or not follow; but this very imagination is itself within the stream, for there is no way other than the Way. Willy-nilly, we are it and go with it. From a strictly logical point of view, this means nothing and gives us no information. Tao is just a name for whatever happens, or, as Lao-tzu put it, "The  Tao principle is what happens of itself [tzu-jan]."

It is thus that the *Tao Te Ching* opens with the enigmatic words which are usually translated, "The Tao which can be spoken of is not the eternal Tao." [103c] This translation conceals the fact that the ideogram rendered as "be spoken of" is also Tao, because the word is also used with the meaning of "to speak" or "to say," though it may not have had this use in

---

[2] *Wu-men Kuan* 19, tr. auct. In this context *hsin* must be translated as "consciousness" rather than "mind," "thought," or "heart." But even this is inadequate. "Ordinary consciousness" is the way the world is felt naturally, as by a child who does not yet know how to talk.

the —3rd century. Literally, the passage says, "Tao can be Tao not eternal [or regular] Tao." Many translations are therefore possible:

The Tao that can be told of is not the Absolute Tao (Lin Yutang).

The Way that can be told of is not an Unvarying Way (Waley).

The Tao that is the subject of discussion is not the true Tao (Old).

The Way that may truly be regarded as the Way is other than a permanent way (Duyvendak).[3]

The Flow that can be followed is not the eternal Flow (auct.).

The course that can be discoursed is not the eternal Course (auct.).

The Force that is forced isn't true Force (auct.).

The Tao that can be *tao*-ed is not the invariable Tao (Fung Yu-lan [Bodde]).

In an early form, the ideogram for *tao* shows the moving sign (the crossroads) enclosing a head, though the radical in later times became *cho*, moving step by step, rather than *hsing*, to walk or march.[4] We should probably think of *cho* as "going and pausing" (Wieger [1], p. 789), and thus as "rhythmic movement," where going is *yang* and pausing is *yin*. Thus in the ideogram for Tao *cho* is combined with *shou*, the head,

[3] Note the interesting divergence of Duyvendak (1) from the other versions. He justifies this (pp. 17–19) by pointing out that neither Lao-tzu nor Chuang-tzu uses *tao* with the meaning of "speech," and suggests that the phrase *ch'ang tao* should not be understood as the true, eternal, and authentic Tao, but, on the contrary, as a Tao which is fixed and definable, and thus not the true Tao at all. Following his idea, I would translate, "The Tao which is truly Tao is not a fixed Tao." But doesn't it all come to the same thing?

[4] The pandits are here confused. Wieger (1) sees *hsing* as deriving from a pictogram of the left and right feet (p. 163), whereas Needham (1), p. 222, takes it to be crossroads. In any case, it denotes motion.

and thus Wieger (p. 326) gives Tao the basic meaning of "to go ahead."[5]* One could also think of it as intelligent rhythm. Various translators have called it the Way, Reason, Providence, the Logos, and even God, as in Ware (1), although he is careful to say in his introduction that God = Life and that the word is to be understood in its widest sense.

However, it must be clear from the start that Tao cannot be understood as "God" in the sense of the ruler, monarch, commander, architect, and maker of the universe. The image of the military and political overlord, or of a creator external to nature, has no place in the idea of Tao.

> The great Tao flows [*fan,* also "floats" and "drifts"] every-
> where,
> to the left and to the right,
> All things depend upon it to exist,
> and it does not abandon them.
> To its accomplishments it lays no claim.
> It loves and nourishes all things,
> but does not lord it over them.[6] [103*d*]

Yet the Tao is most certainly the ultimate reality and energy of the universe, the Ground of being and nonbeing.

> The Tao has reality and evidence, but no action and no form. It may be transmitted but cannot be received. It may be attained but cannot be seen. It exists by and through itself. It existed before heaven and earth, and indeed for all eternity. It causes the gods to be divine and the world to be produced. It is above the zenith, but is not high. It is be-

[5] Thus when the Ch'an master Yün-men was asked, "What is the Tao?" he answered with the single word *ch'ü:* go, go on, walk on, go away. This has the sense of going right along without stickiness or hesitation, as in the phrase *mo chih ch'ü.*

* The character *fa* 法 , which means law, or the universal way in Taoism and Buddhism, is simply the two characters 氵 , water, and 去 , go, combined. Therefore, the Chinese equivalent of the title *Tao: The Watercourse Way* would be telegraphically translated as *Tao-Water/ Go-Flowing-Water.*

[6] *Lao-tzu* 34, tr. auct.

neath the nadir, but is not low. Though prior to heaven and
earth, it is not ancient. Though older than the most ancient,
it is not old.[7] [70*a*]

The imagery associated with the Tao is maternal, not paternal.

> There is something obscure which is complete
> before heaven and earth arose;
> tranquil, quiet,
> standing alone without change,
> moving around without peril.
> It could be the mother of everything.
> I don't know its name,
> and call it Tao.[8] [103*e*]

Far from being the active agent, the subject of the verb, the
doer and maker of things, "the Tao does [*wei,* also "makes"]
nothing, but nothing is left undone." [102*a*] It has the power of
passivity for which women have always been celebrated, and
one might say that its gravity is its energy.

> Know the male, but keep the female,
> so becoming a universal river-valley.
> Being the universal river-valley,
> one has the eternal virtue [*te*] undivided
> and becomes again as a child.[9]

> The heavy is the origin of the light;
> (or, Gravity is the root of lightness;)
> the quiet is master of the hasty.[10] [102*b*]

Thus the Tao is the course, the flow, the drift, or the process
of nature, and I call it the Watercourse Way because both
Lao-tzu and Chuang-tzu use the flow of water as its principal
metaphor. But it is of the essence of their philosophy that the

---

[7] *Chuang-tzu* 6, tr. Fung Yu-lan (3), p. 117, mod. auct. Note the
sophisticated distinction between eternity and everlasting time, and the contrast with the image of the Father-God as the Ancient of Days.

[8] *Lao-tzu* 25, tr. auct.

[9] *Lao-tzu* 28, tr. auct.

[10] *Lao-tzu* 26, tr. auct.

Tao cannot be defined in words and is not an idea or concept. As Chuang-tzu says, "It may be attained but not seen," or, in other words, felt but not conceived, intuited but not categorized, divined but not explained. In a similar way, air and water cannot be cut or clutched, and their flow ceases when they are enclosed. There is no way of putting a stream in a bucket or the wind in a bag. Verbal description and definition may be compared to the latitudinal and longitudinal nets which we visualize upon the earth and the heavens to define and enclose the positions of mountains and lakes, planets and stars. But earth and heaven are not cut by these imaginary strings. As Wittgenstein said, "Laws, like the law of causation, etc., treat of the network and not of what the network describes."[11] For the game of Western philosophy and science is to trap the universe in the networks of words and numbers, so that there is always the temptation to confuse the rules, or laws, of grammar and mathematics with the actual operations of nature. We must not, however, overlook the fact that human calculation is *also* an operation of nature, but just as trees do not represent or symbolize rocks, our thoughts—even if intended to do so—do not necessarily represent trees and rocks. Thoughts grow in brains as grass grows in fields. Any correspondence between them is abstract, as between ten roses and ten stones, which does not take into account the smell and color of the roses or the shapes and structures of the stones. Although thought is in nature, we must not confuse the game-rules of thought with the patterns of nature.

自然 Now the Chinese, and Taoist, term which we translate as "nature" is *tzu-jan*, meaning the spontaneous, that which is so of itself. We might call it the automatic or automotive were it not that these words are associated with mechanisms and artifacts which are not truly "so" of themselves. Nature as *tzu-jan* might be taken to mean that everything grows and op-

11 Wittgenstein (1), 6.35. Cf. also 6.341-2.

erates independently, on its own, and to be the meaning of the verse:

> (As I) sit quietly, doing nothing,
> Spring comes and grass grows of itself.[12]

But it is basic to the Taoist view of the world that every thing-event (*shih* or *wu*) is what it is only in relation to all others. The earth, and every tiniest thing upon it, inevitably "goes-with" the sun, moon, and stars. It needs them just as much as it needs, and consists of, its own elements. Conversely, the sun would not be light without eyes, nor would the universe "exist" without consciousness—and vice versa. This is the principle of "mutual arising" (*hsiang sheng*) which is explained in the second chapter of the *Tao Te Ching*.[13]

事物

相生

The principle is that if everything is allowed to go its own way the harmony of the universe will be established, since every process in the world can "do its own thing" only in relation to all others. The political analogy is Kropotkin's anarchism—the theory that if people are left alone to do as they please, to follow their nature and discover what truly pleases them, a social order will emerge of itself. Individuality is inseparable from community. In other words, the order of nature is not a forced order; it is not the result of laws and commandments which beings are compelled to obey by external violence, for in the Taoist view there really is no obdurately external world. My inside arises mutually with my outside, and though the two may differ they cannot be separated.

Thus everything's "own way" is the "own way" of the uni-

---

[12] Quoted in *Zenrin Kushu* (*Ch'an Ling Chü Chi*), p. 194, tr. auct. This is a small book of sayings often used in Zen (Ch'an) Buddhist teaching. It consists of short verses ranging from one single word to nearly thirty, usually rhyming easily as in poetry. This particular saying is a ten-word verse divided into two five-word couplets.

[13] See above, pp. 22–23. Also *Chuang-tzu*, below, p. 52.

verse, of the Tao. Because of the mutual interdependence of all beings, they will harmonize if left alone and not forced into conformity with some arbitrary, artificial, and abstract notion of order, and this harmony will emerge *tzu-jan*, of itself, without external compulsion. No organization, in the political and commercial sense of the word, is organic. Organizations, in this sense, are based on the following of linear rules and laws imposed from above—that is, of strung-out, serial, one-thing-at-a-time sequences of words and signs which can never grasp the complexity of nature, although nature is only "complex" in relation to the impossible task of translating it into these linear signs. Outside the human world, the order of nature goes along without consulting books—but our human fear is that the Tao which cannot be described, the order which cannot be put into books, is chaos.

If Tao signifies the order and course of nature, the question is, then, what *kind* of order? Lao-tzu (ch. 25) does indeed use the term *hun*—obscure, chaotic, turgid—for the state of the Tao before heaven and earth arose, but I do not think that this can mean chaos in the sense of mess and disorder such as we see when things formerly organized are broken up. It has rather the sense of *hsüan,* of that which is deep, dark, and mysterious prior to any distinction between order and disorder—that is, before any classification and naming of the features of the world.

> The un-named is heaven and earth's origin;
> Naming is the mother of ten thousand things.
> Whenever there is no desire (or, intention),
>     one beholds the mystery;
> Whenever there is desire, one beholds the manifestations.
> These two have the same point of departure,
>     but differ (because of) the naming.
> Their identity is *hsüan*—
>     *hsüan* beyond *hsüan,* all mystery's gate.[14] [102c]

14 *Lao-tzu* 1, tr. auct.

The "chaos" of *hsüan* is the nature of the world before any distinctions have been marked out and named, the wiggly Rorschach blot of nature. But as soon as even one distinction has been made, as between *yin* and *yang* or 0 and 1, all that we call the laws or principles of mathematics, physics, and biology follow of necessity, as has recently been demonstrated in the calculus system of G. Spencer Brown (1). But this necessity does not appear to be a compulsion or force outside the system itself. In other words, the order of the Tao is not an obedience to anything else. As Chuang-tzu says, "It exists by and through itself"; it is *sui generis* (self-generating), *zu-jan* (of itself so), and has the property of that forgotten attribute of God called aseity—that which is *a* (by) *se* (itself). But in the case of the Tao the form of its order is not only free from any external necessity; also, it does not impose its rule on the universe, as if the Tao and the universe were separate entities. In short, the order of the Tao is not law.

The Chinese word *tse* comes closer than any other to what we mean by positive law—to the laying down and following of written rules and lists of what may and may not be done, to going by the book. Thus we read in the *Huai Nan Tzu* book: 則

> The Tao of Heaven operates mysteriously [*hsüan*] and secretly; it has no fixed shape; it follows no definite rules [*wu-tse*]; it is so great that you can never come to the end of it; it is so deep that you can never fathom it.[15]

But though the Tao is *wu-tse* (nonlaw), it has an order or pattern which can be recognized clearly but not defined by the book because it has too many dimensions and too many variables. This kind of order is the principle of *li*, a word

無則

理

---

[15] *Huai Nan Tzu* 9, p. 1b, tr. Needham (1), vol. 2, p. 561.

which has the original sense of such patterns as the markings in jade or the grain in wood.[16]

*Li* may therefore be understood as organic order, as distinct from mechanical or legal order, both of which go by the book. *Li* is the asymmetrical, nonrepetitive, and unregimented order which we find in the patterns of moving water, the forms of trees and clouds, of frost crystals on the window, or the scattering of pebbles on beach sand. It was through the appreciation of *li* that landscape painting arose in China long before Europeans got the point of it, so that now painters and photographers show us constantly the indefinable beauty of such lilts as waterfalls and bubbles in foam. Even abstract and nonobjective paintings have the same forms that may be found in the molecules of metals or the markings on shells. As soon as this beauty is pointed out it is immediately recognized, though we cannot say just why it appeals to us. When aestheticians and art critics try to explain it by showing works of art with Euclidean diagrams superimposed on them—supposedly to demonstrate elegance of proportion or rhythm—they simply make fools of themselves. Bubbles do not interest one merely because they congregate in hexagons or have measurable surface tensions. Geometrization always reduces natural form to something less than itself, to an oversimplification and rigidity which screens out the dancing curvaceousness of nature. It seems that rigid people feel some basic disgust with wiggles; they cannot dance without seeing a diagram of the steps, and feel that swinging the hips is obscene. They want to "get things straight," that is, in linear order, which is *tse* but not *li*.

---

[16] Cf. Needham (1), vol. 2, sec. 18.7. This whole section is a marvelous discussion of the differences between Western and Chinese views of law, both human and natural. Though the mature philosophy of *li* was formulated by Chu Hsi (+1130 to +1200), the word appears thirty-five times in the *Chuang-tzu* book.

But who can straighten out water? Water is the essence of life and is therefore Lao-tzu's favorite image of the Tao.

The highest good is like water,
for the good of water is that it nourishes everything without
    striving.
It occupies the place which all men think bad
    [i.e., the lowest level].[17] [102*d*]

It is thus that Tao in the world is like a
    river going down the valley to the ocean.[18] [102*e*]

The most gentle thing in the world overrides the most hard.[19]
    [102*g*]

How do coves and oceans become kings of a hundred rivers?
Because they are good at keeping low—
That is how they are kings of the hundred rivers.[20] [102*f*]

Nothing in the world is weaker than water,
But it has no better in overcoming the hard.[21] [101*a*]

So also in Chuang-tzu:

> When water is still, it is like a mirror, reflecting the beard and
> the eyebrows. It gives the accuracy of the water-level, and
> the philosopher makes it his model. And if water thus derives
> lucidity from stillness, how much more the faculties of the
> mind? The mind of the Sage being in repose becomes the
> mirror of the universe, the speculum of all creation.[22] [59*a*]

> The fluidity of water is not the result of any effort on the part
> of the water, but is its natural property. And the virtue of the
> perfect man is such that even without cultivation there is
> nothing which can withdraw from his sway. Heaven is na-
> turally high, the earth is naturally solid, the sun and moon
> are naturally bright. Do they cultivate these attributes?[23] [63*b*]

Chuang-tzu tells also the story of seeing an old man fall into a cataract and come out safely downstream. Asked for an explanation the old man says:

[17] *Lao-tzu* 8, tr. auct.
[18] *Lao-tzu* 32, tr. auct.
[19] *Lao-tzu* 43, tr. auct.
[20] *Lao-tzu* 66, tr. auct.
[21] *Lao-tzu* 78, tr. auct.
[22] *Chuang-tzu* 13, tr. H. A. Giles (1),
    pp. 157–58.
[23] *Chuang-tzu* 21, tr. H. A. Giles (1), p. 268.

No, . . . I have no way [of doing this]. There was my original condition to begin with; then habit growing into nature; and lastly acquiescence in destiny. Plunging in with the whirl, I come out with the swirl. I accommodate myself to the water, not the water to me. And so I am able to deal with it after this fashion. . . . I was born upon dry land . . . and accommodated myself to dry land. That was my original condition. Growing up on the water, I accommodated myself to the water. That was what I meant by nature. And doing as I did without being conscious of any effort so to do, that was what I meant by destiny.[24] [67a]

The patterns of flowing water have been shown by Schwenk (1), Kepes (1), and Huyghe (1) to be memorialized in muscle, bone, wood, and stone, and to have found their way into human art from very early times. In watching its flow we can never find an aesthetic mistake; it is invariably graceful in the wave, the flying spray, or the merest trickle. We ourselves are at least eighty percent water, and for this reason the Taoists feel that it should serve as our model, as witness this remarkable passage from the *Kuan-tzu** book (late —4th century):

管子

Water is the blood of the Earth, and flows through its muscles and veins. Therefore it is said that water is something that has complete faculties. . . . It is accumulated in Heaven and Earth, and stored up in the various things (of the world). It comes forth in metal and stone, and is concentrated in living creatures. Therefore it is said that water is something spiritual. Being accumulated in plants and trees, their stems gain their orderly progression from it, their flowers

[24] *Chuang-tzu* 19, tr. H. A. Giles (1), pp. 239–40. Cf. *Lieh-tzu* 2 and 8.
* *Kuan-tzu*, a collection of works by Kuan Chung, a statesman of pre-Confucian times (d. —645), was put together by the scholars of Chi-Hsia Academy (—300) with later Han interpretations. Some of the most penetrating statements of the Tao can be found in this miscellaneous source volume. Alan Watts had often spoken about doing a book on *Kuan-tzu* and *Huai Nan Tzu,* another mixed source book compiled by scholars at the court of Liu An (d. —122). See selections from both in Needham (1) and in Fung Yu-lan (1); also in *Kuan Tzu*, a two-volume book by W. Allyn Rickett of the University of Pennsylvania, and in *Tao the Great Luminant*, by Evan Morgan.

obtain their proper number, and their fruits gain their proper measure. The bodies of birds and beasts, through having it, become fat and large; their feathers and hair become luxuriant, and their stripes and markings are made apparent. The reason why creatures can realize their potentialities and grow to the norm is that the inner regulation of their water is in accord. . . .

Man is water, and when the producing elements of male and female unite, liquid flows into forms. . . . Thus water becomes accumulated in jade, and the nine virtues appear. It congeals to form man, and his nine openings and five viscera appear. This is its refined essence. . . . What is it, then, that has complete faculties? It is water. There is not one of the various things which is not produced through it. It is only he who knows how to rely (on its principles) who can act correctly. . . .

Hence the solution for the Sage who would transform the world lies in water. Therefore when water is uncontaminated, men's hearts are upright. When water is pure, the people's hearts are at ease. Men's hearts being upright, their desires do not become dissolute. The people's hearts being upright, their conduct is without evil. Hence the Sage, when he rules the world, does not teach men one by one, or house by house, but takes water as his key.[25]

To sum up thus far, Tao is the flowing course of nature and the universe; *li* is its principle of order which, following Needham, we can best translate as "organic pattern"; and water is its eloquent metaphor. But we cannot explain *li* by laying it out flat, as in a geometrical diagram, or define it in the linear order of words, although I am paradoxically trying to do so. Another reason why the Tao and its pattern escape us is that they are ourselves, and we are

> Like a sword that cuts but cannot cut itself;
> Like an eye that sees but cannot see itself.[26]

By watching the nucleus we change its behavior, and in our observing the galaxies they run away from us—and, in trying

25 *Kuan-tzu* 39, tr. Fung Yu-lan (Bodde) (1), vol. 1, pp. 166–67.
26 *Zenrin Kushu* 14, p. 267, tr. auct.

to figure out the brain, the obstacle is that we have no finer instrument than the brain itself for the purpose. The greatest hindrance to objective knowledge is our own subjective presence. There is nothing for it, then, but to trust and go with the Tao as the source and ground of our own being which "may be attained but not seen."

Is there any clear way of distinguishing organic pattern from mechanical and linear pattern, between nature and artifice, growing and making? Obviously, no animal or plant is *made* in the same way that a table is made of wood. A living creature is not an assemblage of parts, nailed, screwed, or glued together. Its members and organs are not assembled from distant sources and gathered to a center. A tree is not made of wood; it is wood. A mountain is not made of rock; it is rock. The seed grows into the plant by an expansion from within, and its parts or distinguishable organs develop simultaneously as it expands. Certainly, the growing seed is gathering nourishment from its environment, but the process is no mere sticking together of the nutritive elements, for it absorbs and transforms them, and one sees nothing like this in the manufacture of an electric motor or computer. Though we talk about the mechanisms of organisms, surely this is no more than analogy. In studying organisms by the analytic way of breaking them down into parts we are simply using a mechanical image of their structure. Such analysis is the linear, bit-by-bit method of conscious attention, whereas in the living organism the so-called "parts" are exfoliated simultaneously throughout its body. Nature has no "parts" except those which are distinguished by human systems of classification, and it is only by elaborate surgery that any part of a body can be replaced. The body is not a surgical construct put together with scalpels, clamps, and sutures. We must make a distinction between an organism which is differentiated and a machine which is partitive. Machines generating other machines will always do so by assemblage and the linear method, although we are coming to the point of combining such machines as computers with organic elements. In fact the computer was always combined with an organic element—man himself, for man is the boss and creator of the computer.

But the Tao is not considered the boss and creator of our organic universe. It may reign but it does not rule. It is the pattern of things but not the enforced law. Thus we read in the *Han Fei Tzu* book (early —3rd century):

> Tao is that whereby all things are so, and with which all principles agree. Principles (*li*) are the markings (*wen*) of completed things. Tao is that whereby all things become complete. Therefore it is said that Tao is what gives principles. When things have their principles, the one (thing) cannot be the other. . . . All things have each their own different principle, whereas Tao brings the principles of all things into single agreement. Therefore it can be both one thing and another, and is not in one thing only.[27]

韓非子
理 紋

This is, again, analogous to Kropotkin's anarchy. If each thing follows its own *li* it will harmonize with all other things following theirs, not by reason of rule imposed from above but by their mutual resonance (*ying*) and interdependence.

應

The Taoists are saying, then, that seen as a whole the universe is a harmony or symbiosis of patterns which cannot exist without each other. However, when it is looked at section by section we find conflict. The biological world is a mutual eating society in which every species is the prey of another. But if there were any species not preyed upon by another, it would increase and multiply to its own self-strangulation, as human beings, through their skill in defeating other species (such as bacteria), are in danger of disrupting

[27] *Han Fei Tzu* 20, tr. Fung Yu-lan (Bodde) (1), vol. 1, p. 177.

the whole biological order by overpopulation and thus of destroying themselves. For this reason anyone who sets out to govern the world puts everything, and especially himself, in danger.

> Those who would take over the world and manage it,
> I see that they cannot grasp it;
> for the world is a spiritual [shen] vessel
> and cannot be forced.
> Whoever forces it spoils it.
> Whoever grasps it loses it.[28] [101b]

In the light of this passage from Lao-tzu we must look at the critical section in Chuang-tzu in which the government or regulation of the world and its organisms is discussed. Having first drawn an analogy between the different sounds which various holes and apertures evoke from the wind, and the changing moods, emotions, and thoughts of the human heart, Chuang-tzu goes on to say:

> If there is no other, there will be no I. If there is no I, there will be none to make distinctions. This seems to be true. But what causes these varieties? It might seem as if there would be a real Lord, but there is no indication of His existence. One may believe that He exists, but we do not see His form. He may have reality, but no form. The hundred parts of the human body, with its nine openings, and six viscera, all are complete in their places. Which shall I prefer? Do you like them all equally? Or do you like some more than others? Are they all servants? Are these servants unable to control each other, but need another as ruler? Do they become rulers and servants in turn? Is there any true ruler other than themselves?[29] [73a]

[28] *Lao-tzu* 29, tr. auct. *Shen* presents problems for the translator, for the usually chosen meanings—spirit, god, divine, supernatural, etc.—are unsatisfactory. I take it to mean that innate intelligence (or *li*) of each organism in particular and of the universe as a whole which is beyond the reach of calculation.

[29] *Chuang-tzu* 2, tr. Fung Yu-lan (3), pp. 46–47. But see how other translators render the last sentence. "It would seem as though there must be some True Lord among them" (Watson [1]). "Surely there is some soul which sways them all" (H. A. Giles [1]). "I promise you that there is

Just as every point on the surface of a sphere may be seen as the center of the surface, so every organ of the body and every being in the cosmos may be seen as its center and ruler.

This is like the Hindu-Buddhist principle of karma—that everything which happens to you is your own action or doing. Thus in many states of mystical experience or cosmic consciousness the difference between what you do and what happens to you, the voluntary and the involuntary, seems to disappear. This feeling may be interpreted as the sense that everything is voluntary—that the whole universe is your own action and will. But this can easily flip into the sense that everything is involuntary. The individual and the will are nothing, and everything that might be called "I" is as much beyond control as the spinning of the earth in its orbit. But from the Taoist standpoint these two views fall short. They are polar ways of seeing the same truth: that there is no ruler and nothing ruled. What goes on simply happens of itself (*tzu-jan*) without either push or pull, since every push is also a pull and every pull a push, as in using a steering wheel. This is, then, a transactional view of the world, for as there is no buying without selling, and vice versa, there is no environment without organisms, and vice versa. This is, again, the principle of "mutual arising" (*hsiang sheng*). As the universe produces our consciousness, our consciousness evokes the universe; and this realization transcends and closes the debate between materialists and idealists (or mentalists), determinists and free-willers, who represent the *yin* and the *yang* of philosophical opinion.

Many would object that this view of the universe abrogates the basic law of cause and effect, as when we think that lack

___

a real sovereign there" (Ware [1]). "There must be a true Ruler among them" (Legge [1]). I would read it as, "Their true ruler is just in this"—referring to the previous sentence, "Do they become rulers and servants in turn?"

of rain causes a drought, and a drought causes famine, and famine causes death. But lack of rain, drought, famine, and death are simply four ways of looking at, and describing, the same event. Given living organisms, lack-of-rain = death. The notion of causality is simply a lame way of connecting the various stages of an event which we have distinguished and separated for purposes of description; so that, beguiled by our own words, we come to think of these stages as different events which must be stuck together again by the glue of causality. In fact, the only single event is the universe itself. *Li,* not causality, is the rationale of the world.[30]

If we try to sort the ideas of Taoism into the categories of Western thought, it appears that what we have here is a naturalistic pantheism in which the Tao—not being a personal God—must therefore be an unconscious though nonetheless formative energy, like a magnetic field. As I understand formal pantheism, it is the idea that the universe, considered as a mass of distinct things and events, is simply God by another name, so that calling it God adds nothing to it, except perhaps a certain attitude of awe and respect. But although Taoists speak of the universe (in the common Chinese way) as *wan wu,* the "ten thousand things," this does not imply that it is simply a sum of separate objects. Things (*wu*) are not so much entities as differentiations or forms (cf. the Sanskrit *rupa*) in the unified field of the Tao. This follows necessarily from the principle of mutual arising.

萬物

> The knowledge of the ancients was perfect. How perfect?
> At first, they did not know that there were things. This is
> the most perfect knowledge; nothing can be added. Next,

[30] Shortly before his death in 1972, Lancelot Law Whyte, the British morphologist and philosopher of science, explained to me that he was working on the idea that the angular measurement of patterns was a far more effective way of describing the world than the measurement of the action and reaction of pressures and forces. His work relevant to this theme is in the Bibliography.

they knew that there were things, but did not yet make distinctions between them. Next, they made distinctions between them, but they did not yet pass judgments upon them. When judgments were passed, Tao was destroyed.[31] [72*a*]

And again:

The universe came into being with us together; with us, all things are one.[32] [73*b*]

Furthermore, to conceive the Tao as an unconscious energy is as much off the point as to conceive it as a personal ruler or God. But if, as is the case, the Tao is simply inconceivable, what is the use of having the word and of saying anything at all about it? Simply because we know intuitively that there is a dimension of ourselves and of nature which eludes us because it is too close, too general, and too all-embracing to be singled out as a particular object. This dimension is the ground of all the astonishing forms and experiences of which we are aware. Because we are aware, it cannot be unconscious, although we are not conscious *of* it—as of an external thing. Thus we can give it a name but cannot make any definitive statement about it—as we saw to be the case with whatever it is that is named "electricity." Our only way of apprehending it is by watching the processes and patterns of nature, and by the meditative discipline of allowing our minds to become quiet, so as to have vivid awareness of "what is" without verbal comment.

The baby looks at things all day without squinting and staring; that is because his eyes are not focused on any particular object. He goes without knowing where he is going, and stops without knowing what he is doing. He merges himself with the surroundings and goes along with them. These are the principles of mental hygiene.[33] [64*b*]

[31] *Chuang-tzu* 2, tr. Fung Yu-lan (3), p. 53.
[32] Ibid., p. 56.
[33] *Chuang-tzu* 23, tr. Lin Yutang (3), p. 86, mod. auct.

也道也者不可須臾離也可離非道

無門關第十九

南泉因趙州問如何是道泉云平

常心是道州云還可趣向否泉云

擬向即乖州云不擬爭知是道泉

云道不屬知不屬不知知是妄覺

不知是無記若真達不疑之道猶

如太虛廓然洞豁豈可強是非

州於言下頓悟 [b '38]

56

莊子駢拇

且夫待鉤繩規矩而正者是削其
性繩約膠漆而固者是侵其德也
屈折礼乐呴俞仁義以慰天下之
心者此失其常然也天下有常然
常然者曲者不以鉤直者不以繩
圓者不以規方者不以矩附離不
以膠漆約束不以繩索

[a: 110]

莊子刻意

吹呴呼吸吐故納新熊經鳥申為
壽而已矣此道引之士養形之人

57

蓋師是而非師治而弄亂乎是

未明天地之理萬物之情者也是

猶師天而子地師陰而子陽乎不

可引以失然亚語而不舍亂思則

誣也

[a: 26]

知道者不達於理達於理者不明

於權明於權者不以物害己五德

者火弗能熱水弗能溺寒暑弗能

害禽獸弗能賊非謂其薄之也言

察乎安危寧於禍福謹於去就莫

之能害也

[b: 116]

58

莊子天道

水靜則明燭鬚眉平中準大匠取

[a: 47]

法焉水靜猶明而況精神

斲輪徐則甘而不固疾則苦而不
入不徐不疾得之於手而應於心
口不能言有數存焉於其間臣不
能以喻臣之子臣之子亦不能受
之於臣是以行年七十而老斲輪

[b: 112]

莊子山木

材與不材之間似之而非也故未
免乎累若夫乘道德而浮游則不
然無譽無訾一龍一蛇與時俱化
而無肯專為一上一下以和為量
浮游乎萬物之祖物物而不物於
物則胡可得而累邪 [a: 97]

汝哉形莫若緣情莫若率緣
則不離率則不勞不離不勞 [b: 98]

莊子養生

適來夫子時也適去夫子順也安
時而處順哀樂不能入也古者謂
是帝之縣觀指窮於為薪火傳也
不知其盡也

[a: 114]

莊子人間世

一若志无聽之以耳而聽之以心
无聽之以心而聽之以氣聽止於
耳心止於符氣也者虛而待物者
也唯道集虛虛者心齋也

[b: 117]

德人者居无思引无虑不藏是抛

[a: 80]

美豈四海之内共利之之謂悅共

給之之謂安怡乎萬嬰兒之失乎

毋父懷乎萬引而失乎道此財用

有餘而不知乎此有來飲食取之

而不知乎此從

玉治之垂不尚賢不使能上尊樗

枝民為野麓端正而不知以為義

相愛而不知以為仁實而不知以

為忠當而不知以為信蠢勤而相

使不以為賜是故引而无逵事而

无傳

莊子在宥

聞在宥天下不聞治天下也在之
也者恐天下之淫其性也宥之也
者恐天下之遷其德也天下不淫
其性不遷其德有治天下者哉

[a: 81]

莊子田子方

夫水之於汋也无為而才自然矣
至人之於德也不修而物不能離
焉若天之自高地之自厚日月之
自明夫何修焉

[b: 47]

63

齕草飲水翹足而陸此馬之真性
火燒之剔之刻之雒之連之以羈
馽編之以皁棧馬有橛飾之患而
後有鞭筴之威此亦治天下者之
過也

[a: 115]

莊子庚桑楚

終日視而目不瞚偏不在外也行
不知所往居不知所為與物委蛇
而同其波是衛生之經已

[b: 55]

梓慶削木為鐻，鐻成，見者驚猶鬼
神。魯侯見而問焉，曰："子何術以為
焉？"對曰："臣工人，何術之有！雖然，有
一焉：臣將為鐻，未嘗敢以耗氣也，
必齊以靜心。齊三日，而不敢懷慶
嘗爵祿；齊五日，不敢懷非譽巧拙；
齊七日，輒然忘吾有四肢形體也。
當是時也，無公朝，其巧專而外骨
消；然後入山林，觀天性形軀，至矣，
然後成見鐻，然後加手焉；不然則
已。則以天合天，器之所以疑神者，

[10]

以心稽故至靈臺一而不桎

[a: 110]

顏淵問仲尼曰吾嘗濟乎觴深之
淵津人操舟若神吾問焉曰操舟
可學邪曰可善游者數能若乃夫
没人則未嘗見舟而便操之也吾
問焉而不吾告敢問何謂邪仲尼
曰善游者數能忘水也若乃夫没
人未嘗見舟而便操之也彼視淵
若陵視舟之覆猶其車卻也覆卻
萬方陳乎前而不得入其舍惡往

而不暇

[b: 111]

66

莊子達生

止吾先道吾始乎故長乎性成乎

命與齊俱入與汩偕出從水之道

而不為私焉此吾所以蹈之也

吾生於陵而安於陵故也長於水

而安於水性也不知吾所以然而

然命也 [a: 48]

夫醉者之墜車雖疾不死骨節與

人同而犯害與人異其神全也乘

亦不知也墜亦不知也是故逆物

而不慴彼得全於酒而猶若是而

出不訢不入不距偸然而往偸然
而來而已矣不忘其所始不求其
終受而喜之忘而復之是之謂
不以心捐道不以人助天是之謂
真人

特犯人之形而猶喜之若人之形
者萬化而未始有極也其為樂可
勝計邪故聖人將遊於物之所不
得遯而皆存善妖善老善始善終
人猶効之又況萬物之所係而一
化之所待乎
[b: 87]

68

能外天下已外天下矣吾又守之
七日而後能外物已外物矣吾又
守之九日而後能外生已外生矣
而後能朝徹朝徹而後能見獨見
獨而後能無古今無古今而後能
入於不死不生殺生者不死生生
者不生為物無不將也無不迎也
無不毀也無不成也其名為攖寧
攖寧也者攖而後成者也

[a: 91]

芳兰者无心于霅云窜家不颗颗涛
丝州秋烬丝州寺喜然通口时興

夫道有情有信無為無形可傳而
不可受可得而不可見自本自根
未有天地自古以固存神鬼神帝
生天生地在太極之先而不為高
在六極之下而不為深先天地生
而不為長久於上古而不為老

[a: 40]

夫卜梁得有聖人之才而無聖人
之道我有聖人之道而無聖人之
才吾欲以教之庶幾其果為聖人
乎不然以聖人之道告聖人之才
亦易矣吾猶守而告之參日而後

(continued on p. 69)

予惡乎知說生之非惑邪予惡乎
知惡死之非弱喪而不知歸者邪
予惡乎知夫死者不悔其始之蘄
生乎夢飲酒者旦而哭泣夢哭泣
者旦而田獵方其夢也不知其夢
也夢之中又占其夢焉覺而後知
其夢也且有大覺而後知此其大
夢也而愚者自以為覺竊竊然知
之君乎牧乎固哉丘也與女皆夢
也予謂女夢亦夢也

[a: 93]

71

古之人其知有所至矣惡乎至有

以為未始有物者至矣盡矣不可

以加矣其次以為有物矣而未始

對也其次以為有封焉而未始有

是非也是非之彰也道之所以虧

也

[a: 54]

昔者莊周夢為胡蝶栩栩然胡蝶

也自喻適志與不知周也俄然覺

則蘧蘧然周也不知周之夢為胡

蝶與胡蝶之夢為周與

[b: 93]

莊子齊物論

非彼無我，非我無所取。是亦近矣，而不知其所為使。若有真宰，而特不得其朕。可行己信，而不見其形，有情而無形。百骸、九竅、六藏，賅而存焉，吾誰與為親？汝皆說之乎？其有私焉？如是皆有為臣妾乎？其臣妾不足以相治乎？其遞相為君臣乎？其有真君存焉。

[a: 52]

天地與我並生，萬物與我為一。

[b: 55]

73

# 4. Wu-wei

"THE TAO DOES NOTHING,
and yet nothing is left undone."[1] [101*c*]
These famous words of Lao-tzu
obviously cannot be taken in their literal
sense, for the principle of "nonaction" (*wu-wei*)
is not to be considered inertia, laziness, *laissez-faire,* or
mere passivity. Among the several meanings of *wei* are

[1] *Lao-tzu* 37, tr. auct.

to be, to do, to make, to practice, to act out; and in the form 偽 it means false, simulated, counterfeit. But in the context of Taoist writings it quite clearly means forcing, meddling, and artifice—in other words, trying to act against the grain of *li*. Thus *wu-wei* as "not forcing" is what we mean by going with the grain, rolling with the punch, swimming with the current, trimming sails to the wind, taking the tide at its flood, and stooping to conquer. It is perhaps best exemplified in the Japanese arts of *judo* and *aikido* where an opponent is defeated by the force of his own attack, and the latter art reaches such heights of skill that I have seen an attacker thrown to the floor without even being touched.

理

The principle is illustrated by the parable of the pine and the willow in heavy snow. The pine branch, being rigid, cracks under the weight; but the willow branch yields to the weight, and the snow drops off. Note, however, that the willow is not limp but springy. *Wu-wei* is thus the life-style of one who follows the Tao, and must be understood primarily as a form of intelligence—that is, of knowing the principles, structures, and trends of human and natural affairs so well that one uses the least amount of energy in dealing with them. But this intelligence is, as we have seen, not simply intellectual; it is also the "unconscious" intelligence of the whole organism and, in particular, the innate wisdom of the nervous system. *Wu-wei* is a combination of this wisdom with taking the line of least resistance in all one's actions. It is not the mere avoidance of effort. In *judo*, for example, one uses muscle— but only at the right moment, when the opponent is off balance or has overextended himself. But even this effort has a peculiarly unforced quality which is called *ch'i*, roughly equivalent to the Sanskrit *prana*—an energy associated with breath.

氣

This may be illustrated with the *aikido* exercise of the unbendable arm. The right arm is extended to the front and the opponent is invited to bend it. If the arm is held rigidly, a strong opponent will eertainly bend it. If, on the other hand, it is held out easily, with the eyes fixed on a distant point, and with the feeling that it is a rubber hose through which water is flowing towards that point, it will be extremely difficult to bend. Without straining, one simply assumes that the arm will stay straight, come what may, because of the flow of *ch'i*. During the test, breathe out slowly, as if from the belly, and think of the breath as moving through the arm. This is perhaps a form of what we call, or rather miscall, self-hypnosis, which has nothing to do with sleep. I have found that something of the same kind can be used in opening a stiff cap on a jar, and I knew an old Zen master, frail in appearance, who, seemingly by leaning against them, moved heavy rocks which defeated strong young men.

Just as water follows gravity and, if trapped, rises to find a new outlet, so *wu-wei* is the principle that gravity is energy, and the Taoist finds in gravity a constant stream which may be used in the same way as the wind or a current. Falling with gravity constitutes the immense energy of the earth spinning in its orbit around the sun.

The phrase *wu-wei* was once, and only once, used by Confucius. "The Master said: 'Was it not [the Emperor] Shun who did nothing [*wu-wei*] and yet ruled well? What did he do? He merely corrected his person and took his proper position as ruler.' "[2] The principle, in its political sense, was first discussed at length by Shen Pu-hai (d. −337) in a lost work called the *Shen-tzu* from which only quotations by other authors remain, and which may perhaps be earlier than both the *Lao-tzu* and *Chuang-tzu* books.[3] He explained it simply

2 *Lun-yü* 15.4, tr. Creel (1), p. 58.
3 Concerning whom see Creel (1), pp. 61 ff.

TAO: THE WATERCOURSE WAY

as delegation of authority and of administrative duties, as the noninvolvement of the Emperor in the fussy details of government. In Lao-tzu and Chuang-tzu it means this and much more, for Lao-tzu, in particular, may be interpreted at several different levels. The *Tao Te Ching* may be taken as a manual of advice on government, as a book of natural philosophy, or as a compendium of metaphysical and mystical wisdom. As Creel points out, these early Taoists were writing in the extremely troubled time of the Warring States Period (−403 to −221) when *laissez-faire* in politics would have been suicidal; and yet they were by no means stupid people.

We should look first, then, at the political aspect of *wu-wei*. Reading Lao-tzu and Chuang-tzu as commentary on their own time, they are pointing out the utter folly of ambition for political power, such that it is a burden to those who hold it. As we can clearly see today, no one in his senses would *want* to be the supreme governor of any great nation, for one cannot imagine a more hectic, frustrating, anxiety-ridden, and demanding way of life—where one is never out of reach of the telephone, is constantly accompanied by guards, and must make momentous decisions (on the basis of screened and scanty information) hour after hour. Under such pressure, no one can remain a human being with time to "stand and stare," to wander through the woods with one or two politically unimportant friends, or to sit alone on a beach and watch the sea. Great power is worry, and total power is boredom, such that even God renounces it and pretends, instead, that he is people and fish and insects and plants: the myth of the king who goes wandering among his subjects in disguise.

So Lao-tzu (ch. 60) advises the ruler to govern a state as one cooks a small fish—that is, don't turn it so often in the pan that it disintegrates—and he envisages the ideal state as no bigger than a village.

78

Supposing here is a small state with few people.
Though there may be various mechanical contrivances,
    they will not be used.
People will be well aware of their mortality and not
    overextend themselves.
Though they have boats and carriages they will not
    travel in them;
though they have weapons they will not show them.
They will restore the use of knotted cords (for
    keeping records).
They will be satisfied with their food,
delighted in their clothes,
comfortable in their homes,
and happy with their customs.
Though the neighboring states are within sight,
and their cocks' crowing and dogs' barking within hearing,
the people will not go abroad all their lives.[4] [101*d*]

It must be understood, in passing, that both Lao-tzu and Chuang-tzu enjoy the humor of overstating their case—the latter sometimes choosing truly preposterous examples to illustrate a point. So, in this instance, Lao-tzu is not to be taken absolutely seriously: but he is making the point that people would be much better off if they would curb ambition, slow down the tempo of life, and not despise working with their hands.

Throughout Taoist writing there is a nostalgia for the "true men of ancient times," reminiscent of Rousseau and the idealization of the Noble Savage in the +18th century—a nostalgia which fashionable anthropology has for a long time deplored. But today one wonders. Is a long life such a good thing if it is lived in daily dread of death or in constant search for satisfaction in a tomorrow which never comes? Is technological progress a disease, symptomatic of being unable to be centered in and to enjoy the present? As Chuang-tzu puts it:

---

[4] *Lao-tzu* 80, tr. Ch'u Ta-kao (1), p. 95, mod. auct. Cf. *Chuang-tzu* 10.

The man of perfect virtue in repose has no thoughts, in action no anxiety. He recognizes no right, nor wrong, nor good, nor bad. Within the Four Seas, when all profit—that is his repose. Men cling to him as children who have lost their mothers; they rally around him as wayfarers who have missed their road. He has wealth to spare, but he knows not whence it comes. He has food and drink more than sufficient, but knows not who provides it. . . .

In an age of perfect virtue, good men are not appreciated; ability is not conspicuous. Rulers are mere beacons, while the people are as free as the wild deer. They are upright without being conscious of duty to their neighbors. They love one another without being conscious of charity. They are true without being conscious of loyalty. They are honest without being conscious of good faith. They act freely in all things without recognizing obligations to anyone. Thus, their deeds leave no trace; their affairs are not handed down to posterity.[5] [62a]

Which at once calls to mind a passage from Thoreau:

I saw the setting sun lighting up the opposite side of a stately pine wood. Its golden rays straggled into the aisles of the wood as into some noble hall. I was impressed as if some ancient and altogether admirable and shining family had settled there . . . unknown to me,—to whom the sun was servant,—who had not gone into society in the village,—who had not been called on. I saw their park, their pleasure-ground, beyond through the wood. . . . The pines furnished them with gables as they grew. Their house was not obvious to vision; the trees grew through it. I do not know whether I heard the sounds of a suppressed hilarity or not. They seemed to recline on the sunbeams. They have sons and daughters. They are quite well. The farmer's cart-path, which leads directly through their hall, does not in the least put them out, as the muddy bottom of a pool is sometimes seen through the reflected skies. They . . . do not know

---

[5] *Chuang-tzu* 12, tr. H. A. Giles (1), pp. 151–53, mod. auct. For "They act freely . . . to anyone," Watson (1) gives, "They wriggle around like insects, performing services for one another, but do not know that they are being kind."

that he is their neighbor,—notwithstanding I heard him whistle as he drove his team through the house. Nothing can equal the serenity of their lives. Their coat of arms is simply a lichen. I saw it painted on the pines and oaks. Their attics were in the tops of the trees. They are of no politics. There was no noise of labor. I did not perceive that they were weaving or spinning. Yet I did detect, when the wind lulled and hearing was done away, the finest imaginable sweet musical hum,—as of a distant hive in May, which perchance was the sound of their thinking. They had no idle thoughts, and no one without could see their work, for their industry was not as in knots and excrèscences embayed.[6]

Is such a state of affairs possible, or is this all an idle dream? Remembering that Chuang-tzu exaggerates to make his points, the practical message seems to be that only trouble is made by those who strive to improve themselves and the world by forceful means. "Ah, Liberty—what crimes are committed in thy name!" The idealism of the French, American, and Russian revolutions has always, sooner or later, led to excesses of violence which are justified as being for the liberation and welfare of the peoples molested.

There has been such a thing as letting mankind alone; there has never been such a thing as governing mankind [with success]. Letting alone springs from fear lest men's natural dispositions be perverted and their virtue laid aside. But if their natural dispositions be not perverted nor their virtue laid aside, what room is there left for government?[7] [63a]

When it comes down to it, government is simply an abandonment of responsibility on the assumption that there are people, other than ourselves, who really know how to manage things. But the government, run ostensibly for the good of the people, becomes a self-serving corporation. To keep things under control it proliferates laws of ever-increasing complexity and

[6] Thoreau (1), pp. 628–29.
[7] *Chuang-tzu* 11, tr. H. A. Giles (1), p. 119.

unintelligibility, and hinders productive work by demanding so much accounting on paper that the record of what has been done becomes more important than what has actually been done. About this one might go on and on—but in the current anxiety concerning overpopulation, pollution, ecological imbalance, and the potential disasters of nuclear fission, it is only seldom recognized that governed nations have become self-destroying institutions paralyzed and bogged in their own complications, and suffocated beneath mountains of paper. The Taoist moral is that people who mistrust themselves and one another are doomed.

The further point is that neither an individual nor a society can pull itself up by its own bootstraps, even though it is now commonly being said that this is precisely what we must do. So long as we use force, whether physical or moral, to improve the world and ourselves, we are squandering energy that might otherwise be used for things which *can* be done. This is not the place to go into all the details of these problems. It is only to say that there is basic good sense in the Taoist view that we *must* make the desperate gamble of trusting ourselves and others. However, Lao-tzu makes the reservation, in describing his ideal community, that "though the people have weapons, they do not show them," since weapons are, up to a point, a natural extension of teeth, claws, and shells. The Taoist view of nature was not sentimental. It recognized that violence had sometimes to be used, but always with regret, for

> The best soldier is not soldierly;
> The best fighter is not ferocious.[8] [100a]

In this respect the Confucians and the Taoists were really of one mind. For at the head of all virtues Confucius put, not righteousness (*i*), but human-heartedness (*jen*), which is not so much benevolence, as often translated, but being fully and

[8] *Lao-tzu* 68, tr. Ch'u Ta-kao (1), p. 83.

honestly human—a quality which he refused to define as Lao-
tzu would not define Tao.

> True manhood requires a great capacity and the road thereto
> is difficult to reach. You cannot lift it by your hands and you
> cannot reach it by walking on foot. He who approaches it to
> a greater degree than others may already be called "a true
> man." Now is it not a difficult thing for a man to try to reach
> this standard by sheer effort? Therefore, if the gentle-
> man measures men by the absolute standard of righteous-
> ness [*i*], then it is difficult to be a real man. But if he
> measures by the standard of man, then the better people will
> have some standard to go by. . . .
>   For a long time it has been difficult to find examples of
> true men. Only the superior man can reach that state. There-
> fore the superior man does not try to criticize people for what
> he himself fails in, and he does not put people to shame for
> what they fail in. . . . One who is not a true man cannot
> long stand poverty, nor can he stand prosperity for long. A
> true man is happy and natural in living according to the prin-
> ciples of true manhood, but a [merely] wise man thinks it
> is advantageous to do so. . . . The superior man goes
> through his life without any one preconceived course of ac-
> tion or any taboo. He merely decides for the moment what is
> the right thing to do. . . . The goody-goodies are the thieves
> of virtue.[9]

In other words, a true human* is not a model of righteousness, a prig or a prude, but recognizes that some failings are as
necessary to genuine human nature as salt to stew. Merely
righteous people are impossible to live with because they have
no humor, do not allow the true human nature to be, and are

[9] *Li Chi* 32, tr. Lin Yutang (2), pp. 830–35.
* Note that in the quotation above, the use of such terms as "manhood,"
"gentleman," "a true man," "superior man" is in the tradition in which
"man" denotes human beings of both sexes. In Chinese, the word *jen*
人 , human beings, has no gender differentiation. In the future, I pro-
pose that all translators of Chinese use the word "human" when speaking
of man in this sense. After all, we do not translate the Confucian word
*jen* 仁 as "man-heartedness," but rather as "human-heartedness."

dangerously unconscious of their own shadows. Like all legal-
ists and busybodies, they are trying to put the world on a
Procrustean bed of linear regulations so that they are unable
to make reasonable compromises. In warfare they fight to the
death for unconditional surrender, and, in the name of righteous
principle, will obliterate a territory which they would be better
advised simply to capture and enjoy in a selfish, but much less
harmful, spirit. It is an essential, then, of political *wu-wei*
that one does not try to enforce laws against human nature and
send people to jail for "sins," or crimes without unwilling
victims. Trust in human nature is acceptance of the good-and-
bad of it, and it is hard to trust those who do not admit their
own weaknesses.

For example, let us consider what happened in China when
the Ch'in Dynasty came to power in −221. Its policies were
formulated in the western state of Ch'in as early as −360 by the
Lord Shang.

> All high honors of the state were reserved for the military
> service and for achievements in war. Even the nobles of
> royal blood must be graded anew on the basis of military
> service. Nobles without military distinction were degraded
> to commoners. The objective is to create "a people that looks
> to warfare as a hungry wolf looks at a piece of meat." "If the
> only gate to riches and honor is battle, then when the people
> hear that there is war they will congratulate one another; at
> home and in the street, at their eating and drinking, all the
> songs they sing will be of war." "A ruler who can make the
> people delight in war will become the king of kings." . . .
> To enforce the new laws, the population was organized into
> small groups of five or ten families each, and members of
> each group were required to watch over and report on each
> other. Successful exposure of crime through such spying
> and reporting was to be rewarded on the same scale as kill-
> ing an enemy on the battlefield. Shielding a criminal would

be punished with the same penalty as surrendering to the enemy in war.[10] *

After the Ch'in state had unified all China by conquest, during the period −360 to −221, the Emperor Ch'in Shih Huang Ti went so far as to order the burning of all books not related to strictly practical crafts, and declared, like Hitler, that he was founding a dynasty that would last for a thousand years. But when he died in −210 the people rebelled under the leadership of Liu Pang, who became the Emperor Han Kao Tsu, founder of the Han Dynasty, which endured, with a brief interregnum, for four hundred years (−200 to +200).

> When his revolutionary army triumphantly entered the capital, he called a mass meeting of the elders of the people and declared to them that he knew their long suffering under the tyrannical rule of the Ch'in Empire and would abolish all its repressive laws. So he proclaimed that "hereafter only three simple laws shall prevail: namely, that manslaughter shall be punished by death, and that assault and theft shall be justly punished according to the facts of each case."

[10] Hu Shih, p. 43.

* One of the least spontaneous chores in finishing this book has been the tracking down of titles and page numbers of the sources of Alan's quotations. He never kept account of where and how he found them, at least not on paper. I am grateful to many scholar friends and resourceful librarians who, during the past months, have helped me locate all of them except one. I have decided to let this one go, simply to show that the circle with the open end is generally more real and less sterile. Hu Shih wrote so many different versions of this same historical account in both Chinese and English, and Alan had probably come upon it in the most obscure place—or the most obvious. So far, we have not been able to find it in any of Hu Shih's books that are available in English, or to trace it to any of the articles he contributed to various books and journals on Chinese culture. We do know that he wrote it. All Hu Shih specialists will know where to find it. The others probably couldn't care less.

In my grade-school days, I was once presented to Hu Shih by my father, who knew and admired him. I remember Hu patting me on the head approvingly when I proudly recited by memory a paragraph from his writing, which we were currently studying in our Chinese literature class. Thank you, Uncle Hu, for your contribution to this book.

This early proclaimed policy to relieve the people from the authoritarian rule of too much government was consciously carried out by some of the great statesmen of the Han Empire.

In −201, the second year of the empire, a General Ts'ao, one of the great generals of the revolution, was made governor of the populous and economically advanced state of Ch'i on the eastern coast. He selected an old philosopher to be his chief adviser. This old man was a follower of Lao-tzu and told the Governor that the best way to govern his great state comprising seventy cities was to do nothing and give the people a rest. The Governor religiously carried out his advice throughout his nine years of governorship. The people became prosperous, and his administration was rated the best in the empire. When he was appointed prime minister of the empire in −193, he again practiced his philosophy on a national scale.[11]

When, in −179, the Emperor Wen Ti and his Taoist Empress Tou ascended the throne, they abolished collective family responsibility for crime, punishment by bodily mutilation, and taxes on interstate commerce. They reduced land taxes to a mere thirtieth of the produce, and tried as best they could to avoid warfare on the borders of the empire. Empress Tou persuaded the whole court to read Lao-tzu, and her advice might well be followed by the present potentates of China, Russia, and the United States of America.

> The more restrictions and avoidances are in the empire,
> the poorer become the people.
> The more sharp implements the people keep,
> the more confusions are in the country.
> The more arts and crafts men have,
> the more are frivolous things produced.
> The more laws and regulations are given,
> the more robbers and thieves there are.[12] [100b]

11 Ibid., pp. 44–45.
12 *Lao-tzu* 57, tr. Ch'u Ta-kao (1), p. 72, mod. auct. "Frivolous things" are the kind of objects to be found on sale in "gift shops."

The question now arises whether *wu-wei* and following of the Tao can be cultivated intentionally by some spiritual or psychological discipline such as yoga or *ts'o-ch'an* (Japanese, *za-zen*). Practices of this kind have been in general use among what Creel has termed the Hsien Taoists, discussed at more length in the next chapter. Probably under the influence of Buddhism and other Indian disciplines, these Taoists interested themselves in breath control, sexual yoga, alchemy, and medicine for the purpose of attaining immortality, and established a Taoist church with ordained priests and monasteries. But neither Lao-tzu nor Chuang-tzu had any interest in immorality, and what, if anything, they had to say about formal meditation and the acquisition of psychic powers is minimal.

坐禪

> The True men of old knew nothing of the love of life or of the hatred of death. Entrance into life occasioned them no joy; the exit from it awakened no resistance. Composedly they went and came. They did not forget what their beginning had been, and they did not inquire into what their end would be. They accepted (their life) and rejoiced in it; they forgot (all fear of death), and returned (to their state before life). Thus there was in them the want of any mind to resist the Tao, and of all attempts by means of the Human to resist the Heavenly.[13] [68a]

So far from using any artifice or method to attain spiritual power or to control or rise above the transformations of life and death, Chuang-tzu seems to exult in just going along with the process.

> You have had the nerve to be born human, and you are delighted. But this body undergoes myriads of changes that never come to an end, and does it not thus afford occasion for joys incalculable? Therefore the sage enjoys himself in that from which there is no possibility of separation, and by which all things are preserved. He considers early death or

[13] *Chuang-tzu* 6, tr. Legge (1), p. 286.

> old age, his beginning and his ending, all to be good, and
> in this other men imitate him. How much more will they do
> so in regard to that [Tao] on which all things depend, and
> from which every transformation arises![14] [68b]

In other words, what is ordinarily felt as the wayward, unpredictable, dangerous, and even hostile world—including
one's capricious emotions and inner feelings—is actually one's
own being and doing. The very sense that this is *not* so is, in
turn, part of its being so. Thus from the standpoint of early,
Contemplative Taoism (Creel's term) any deliberate exercise
to cultivate *wu-wei* would seem to be self-contradictory. In
Chuang-tzu's own metaphor, it would be "beating a drum in
search of a fugitive," or, as the Ch'an Buddhists said later,
"putting legs on a snake." In line with Lao-tzu (ch. 38) one
might say, "Superior *wu-wei* does not aim at *wu-wei* and so
it truly is *wu-wei*." Understanding it is a matter of getting the
point intuitively, not a result of some discipline. In the same
way, it does not take any schooling to understand the trick
of representing a third dimension by lines drawn in perspec-
tive; it simply has to be pointed out, and then the experience
of depth in the picture is not just verbal comprehension but
actual vision.

What, then, are we to make of the venerable tradition of
meditative exercises in Hinduism, Buddhism, Hsien Taoism,
and Islamic Sufiism which make cosmic consciousness or
supernormal powers their ostensible goal? If we go ahead to
the early Ch'an writings of the T'ang Dynasty (+618 to
+906), remembering that Ch'an was then a fusion of Taoism
and Buddhism, there can, I think, be no question that such
early Ch'an teachers as Seng-ts'an, Hui-neng, Shen-hui, Ma-
tsu, and even Lin-chi not only laid no stress on meditative
exercises but often dismissed them as irrelevant. Their entire

[14] Ibid., p. 291, mod. auct.

88

直指
問答

emphasis was upon immediate intuitive insight resulting from the teacher's "direct pointing" (*chih-chih*) in question-and-answer interviews called *wen-ta,* by means of which one who had seen into the truth of things simply pointed it out to one who had not—often by nonverbal means, by demonstration rather than explanation.[15] It was for this reason that Hui-neng, the Sixth Patriarch of Ch'an Buddhism (d. +713), called his method "the sudden school," now derided by crypto-Protestant Buddhists as "instant Zen" (like instant coffee)—as if the value of an inspiration or intuition must be judged by the merely quantitative standard of the time and energy spent in preparation for it. How long does it take a child to know that fire is hot?

On the other hand, those who understand the Tao delight, like cats, in just sitting and watching without any goal or result in mind. But when a cat gets tired of sitting, it gets up and goes for a walk or hunts for mice. It does not punish itself or compete with other cats in an endurance test as to how long

[15] In making this point I realize that *vis-à-vis* modern Ch'an (Zen) disciplinarians of the "aching legs" brand of Buddhism, I am a deplorable heretic, since for them *za-zen* (sitting Zen) and *sesshin* (long periods of it) are the *sine qua non* of awakening (or enlightenment) according to their school. I have been sharply reprimanded for this opinion in Kapleau (1), pp. 21–22, 83–84, although the only text he quotes from early Zen literature in refutation is from the *Huang-po Tuan-chi Ch'an-shih Wang-ling Lu* (before +850): "When you practice mind-control [*ts'o-ch'an*], sit in the proper position, stay perfectly tranquil, and do not permit the least movement of your minds to disturb you" (tr. Blofeld [1], p. 131). Considering the vast emphasis laid on *za-zen* in later times, it is strange that this is all Huang-po has to say about it. The reader interested in the roots of this matter has only to consult Hui-neng's *T'an-ching* (tr. Chan Wing-tsit [1] or Yampolsky [1], esp. sec. 19), or the *Shen-hui Ho-chang I-chi* (tr. Gernet [1], esp. sec. 1.111), or Ma-tsu in *Ku-tsun-hsü Yü-lu* (tr. Watts [1], p. 110). For later discussions see Fung Yu-lan (1), vol. 2, pp. 393–406, and Hu Shih. All this evidence corroborates the view that the T'ang masters of Ch'an deplored the use of meditation exercises *as a means* to the attainment of true insight (*wu,* or Japanese *satori*). I had further confirmation of this view in private discussions with D. T. Suzuki and R. H. Blyth, both of whom regarded compulsive "aching legs" *za-zen* as a superstitious fetish of modern Zen practice.

it can remain immovable—unless there is some real reason for being still, such as catching a bird. Contemplative Taoists will happily sit with yogis and Zennists for as long as is reasonable and comfortable, but when nature tells us that we are "pushing the river" we will get up and do something else, or even go to sleep. More than this is certainly spiritual pride. Taoists do not look upon meditation as "practice," except in the sense that a doctor "practices" medicine. They have no design to subjugate or alter the universe by force or will-power, for their art is entirely to go along with the flow of things in an intelligent way. Meditation or contemplation 觀 (*kuan*) develops this intelligence as a by-product, not as a direct objective. The objective or good of contemplation is only that, during a long night,

> The sound of the water
> says what I think.

> His mind is free from all thoughts. His demeanor is still and silent. His forehead beams with simplicity. He is cold as autumn, and warm as spring, for his joy and anger occur as naturally as the four seasons.[16] [69*b*]

Yet it must also be clear that *wu-wei* is not intentional caprice, as when people go out of their way to do whatever is bizarre or unconventional, following convention as slavishly as any square—as their guide for doing its opposite. This was a common misinterpretation of Taoism and Zen when they first became popular among young people in the West. Thus, in fact, Contemplative Taoists do sit in meditation, but not with the egoistic purpose of improving themselves; it is rather that, having understood intuitively that there is no way to go except the way of the Tao "they make excursion into that which things cannot escape" (*Chuang-tzu* 6) and meditate

[16] *Chuang-tzu* 6, tr. Fung Yu-lan (3), p. 113, mod. auct.

for the joy of meditation—the flow of breath, the sound of roosters in the distance, the light on the floor, the susurrus of the wind, the stillness, and, alas, all those things which militant activists of both West and East have, with their frantic purposiveness, learned to disdain. This is the *yin* aspect of the Taoist life, and thus does not exclude—when it becomes timely—the *yang* aspect of delighting in vigor, so that the *t'ai chi chuan* discipline of bodily movement, flowing and swinging, is as much appreciated as sitting in meditation.[17]

太極拳

That Chuang-tzu pointed out the intuitive way of under- standing the Tao without resorting to the artificiality of "spiritual exercises," is stressed by his critic Ko Hung (c. —300), a Hsien Taoist, who termed Chuang-tzu's way as nothing but "pure conversation" (*ch'ing t'an*), or what his modern counterparts might call "mere intellectualization" or nothing but a "head trip." Chuang-tzu, he wrote, "says that life and death are just the same, brands the effort to preserve life as laborious servitude, and praises death as a rest; this doctrine is separated by millions of miles from that of *shen hsien* [holy immortals]."[18]

清談

神仙

The nearest that Chuang-tzu comes to outlining a method of attaining the Tao is put into the mouth of a sage named Nü Chü, presumably a woman:

> There was Pu Liang I, who had the genius of a sage, but not the Tao. I have the Tao, but not the genius. [This surely must be a woman talking.] I wished to teach him, so that he might really become a sage. To teach the Tao of a sage to a man who has the genius, seems to be an easy matter. But no,

[17] It is hard to think of a Western equivalent of *t'ai chi chuan*. Part dance, part physical exercise, and part slow-motion combat, it is nevertheless none of these, but rather, "T'ai chi exemplifies the most subtle principle of Taoism, known as *wu-wei* . . . to act without forcing—to move in ac- cordance with the flow of nature's course . . . and is best understood from watching the dynamics of water" (Huang [1], p. 2).
[18] Creel (1), p. 22.

I kept on telling him; after three days, he began to be able to disregard all worldly matters [i.e., anxieties about status or gain and loss]. After his having disregarded all worldly matters, I kept on telling him; after seven days, he began to be able to disregard all external things [as being separate entities]. After his having disregarded all external things, I kept on telling him; after nine days, he began to be able to disregard his own existence [as an ego]. Having disregarded his own existence, he was enlightened. Having become enlightened, he then was able to gain the vision of the One. Having the vision of the One, he was then able to transcend the distinction of past and present. Having transcended the distinction of past and present, he was then able to enter the realm where life and death are no more. Then, to him, the destruction of life did not mean death, nor the prolongation of life an addition to the duration of his existence. He would follow anything; he would receive anything. To him, everything was in destruction, everything was in construction. This is called tranquillity in disturbance. Tranquillity in disturbance means perfection.[19] [70-69a]

There is a parallel passage in Lieh-tzu where, however, the days are increased to years and the teacher says nothing at all, telling us how Lieh-tzu learned to ride on the wind, or as we would say, walk on air.

At the end of seven years, there was another change. I let my mind reflect on what it would, but it no longer occupied itself with right and wrong. I let my lips utter whatsoever they pleased, but they no longer spoke of profit and loss. . . . At the end of nine years, my mind gave free rein to its reflections, my mouth free passage to its speech. Of right and wrong, profit and loss, I had no knowledge, either as touching myself or others. . . . Internal and External were blended into Unity. After that, there was no distinction between eye and ear, ear and nose, nose and mouth: all were the same. My mind was frozen, my body in dissolution, my flesh and bones all melted together. I was wholly unconscious of what my body was resting on, or what was under my feet. I was

[19] *Chuang-tzu* 6, tr. Fung Yu-lan (3), pp. 119–20.

borne this way and that on the wind, like dry chaff or leaves falling from a tree. In fact, I knew not whether the wind was riding on me or I on the wind.[20]

These passages suggest that *wu-wei* is an almost dreamlike state of consciousness—floating—so that the physical world lacks the hard reality normally present to common sense.

Once upon a time I, Chuang-chou, dreamed that I was a butterfly, a butterfly flying about, enjoying itself. I did not know that it was Chuang-chou. Suddenly I awoke, and veritably was Chuang-chou again. But I do not know whether it was I dreaming that I was a butterfly, or whether I am a butterfly dreaming that I am Chuang-chou.[21] [72*b*]

And again:

How do I know that the love of life is not a delusion? How do I know that he who is afraid of death is not like a man who was away from his home when young and therefore has no intention to return? . . . How do I know that the dead will not repent of their former craving for life? Those who dream of a banquet at night may in the next morning wail and weep. Those who dream of wailing and weeping in the morning go out to hunt. When they dream, they do not know that they are dreaming. In their dream, they may even interpret dreams. Only when they are awake, they begin to know that they dreamed. By and by comes the great awakening, and then we shall find out that life itself is a great dream. All the while, the fools think that they are awake; that they know. With nice discriminations, they make distinctions between princes and grooms. How stupid! Confucius and you are both in a dream. When I say that you are in a dream, I am also in a dream.[22] [71*a*]

The sense that the world is dreamlike, found also in Hinduism and Buddhism, comes mainly from noting its transience

[20] *Lieh-tzu* 2, tr. L. Giles (1), pp. 40–42. It seems that Lieh-tzu is giving physical metaphors for psychological states, and thus that riding on the wind, mind frozen, and body dissolved must not be understood literally.
[21] *Chuang-tzu* 2 ad fin., tr. Fung Yu-lan (3), p. 64, mod. auct.
[22] *Chuang-tzu* 2, tr. Fung Yu-lan (3), pp. 61–62.

rather than from speculations about knowledge and truth, epistemology and ontology, although these come in later. Especially as one grows older, it becomes ever more obvious that things are without substance, for time seems to go by more rapidly so that one becomes aware of the liquidity of solids; people and things become like lights and ripples on the surface of water. We can make fast-motion films of the growth of plants and flowers in which they seem to come and go like gestures of the earth. If we could film civilizations and cities, mountains and stars, in the same way, we would see them as frost crystals forming and dissolving and as sparks on the back of a fireplace. The faster the tempo, the more it would appear that we were watching, not so much a succession of things, as the movement and transformations of one thing—as we see waves on the ocean or the movements of a dancer. In a similar way, what appears through a microscope to be a mass of plastic lumps bristling with spines is, to the naked eye, the clear skin of a girl. Put very crudely, mysticism is the apprehension of one thing doing everything. Taoists put it more subtly so that "doing" does not have the sense of one thing, the Tao, forcing and compelling others.

Generally speaking, the philosophies of the modern West do not take kindly to this dreamlike view of things, perhaps because of the feeling that if we are dreams we are not important, and that if we are not important there is no need to pay each other respect. We have all heard the cliché that human life is cheap in China. Of course, because there is too much of it; and we ourselves are becoming callous as populations multiply and the news media accustom us to the statistics of immense slaughters. No one, however, has demonstrated any necessary relation between people's metaphysical views or religious beliefs and their moral behavior. People who are important can become too important, and thus nuisances to be done away with; and it should be remembered that the tortures and burnings of the Holy Inquisition were committed with deep concern for the fate of heretics' immortal souls.

Often it seems that pain is our measure of reality, for I am not aware that there is ever physical pain in dreams apart from some actual physiological reason. It is thus a common joke that believers in the unreality of matter have difficulty in convincing anyone of the unreality of pain.

> There was a faith-healer of Deal,
> Who said, "Although pain is not real,
>   When the point of a pin
>   Goes into my skin,
> I dislike what I fancy I feel."

Yet the human body contains so much empty space that its ponderable elements could be condensed to the size of that very pinpoint, for its apparent solidity is an illusion arising from the rapid motion of its atomic components—as when a spinning propeller seems to become an impenetrable disk. Perhaps pain is a form of "conditioning," since we know that the type of conditioning called hypnosis can be an extraordinary and selective anaesthetic.

However, let us try to imagine a universe, a realm of experience or a field of consciousness, lacking any extreme which could be called pain or the horrors. Although a fortunate person may pass days, months, and years in most pleasant and comfortable circumstances, there is always an apprehension, a thought in the back of the mind, that pain in some form is at least possible. It lurks around the corner, and he knows that he is fortunate because, all about him, there are those who suffer. All experience, all awareness, seems to be of varied spectra of vibrations so ordered that their extremes, like *yin* and *yang*, must in some way go together. If we cut a bar magnet in halves, so as to take off its north pole, we find only that each half has now north and south poles as before. Thus a universe without the polarity of pleasure and pain would be difficult indeed to imagine. In many societies we have gone a long way towards getting rid of such monstrosities as legal torture and, by medical means, of the pains of disease and surgery. Yet new dreads seem to take their place, and there is always the specter of death in the background.

If, then, we go deep into the very nature of feeling, we begin to see that we do not, and even cannot, want a universe without this polarity. In other words, so long as we desire the experience called pleasure we imply, and so generate, its opposite. Therefore Buddhists and Taoists alike speak of the sage as one who has no desires, though the latter also speak of him as one whose "joy and anger occur as naturally as the four seasons," and here may lie a clue to the problem. For is it even possible not to desire? Trying to get rid of desire is, surely, desiring not to desire.[23] Any project to suppress desire would obviously be contrary to the spirit of *wu-wei,* and implies that "I" am some separate potency which can either subdue desire or be subdued by it. *Wu-wei* is to roll with experiences and feelings as they come and go, like a ball in a mountain stream, though actually there is no ball apart from the convolutions and wiggles of the stream itself. This is called "flowing with the moment," though it can happen only when it is clear that there is nothing else to do, since there is no experience which is not *now.* This now-streaming (*nunc fluens*) is the Tao itself, and when this is clear innumerable

[23] As, of course, the Buddhists very soon found out. It is not usually understood that Buddhism is not so much a doctrine as a dialogue which goes along with a series of experiments. The Buddha did not "teach," as some sort of dogma, that the cure for suffering is the elimination of desire (*trishna*). He simply suggested it as a preliminary experiment, which would, of course and as he surely intended, lead people to see that they were desiring not to desire, and thus involved in a vicious circle.

problems vanish. For so long as there is the notion of ourselves as something different from the Tao, all kinds of tensions build up as between "me" on the one hand, and "experiences" on the other. No action, no force (*wei*) will get rid
of this tension arising from the duality of the knower and the
known, just as one cannot blow away the night. Light, or
intuitive understanding, alone will dissipate the darkness. As
with the ball in the stream, there is no resistance to the up
when now going up, and no resistance to the down when now
going down. To resist is to get seasick.

> A drunken man who falls out of a cart, though he may
> suffer, does not die. His bones are the same as other people's;
> but he meets the accident in a different way. His spirit is in
> a condition of security. He is not conscious of riding in the
> cart; neither is he conscious of falling out of it. Ideas of
> life, death, and fear cannot penetrate his breast; and so he
> does not suffer from contact with objective existences. And
> if such security is to be got from wine, how much more is
> it to be got from Spontaneity.[24] [67*b*]

That was one of Chuang-tzu's charming exaggerations
which he clarifies at other points, as when he distinguishes
between *wu-wei* and holding to the mean, the middle road.

> But halfway between worth and worthlessness, though it
> might seem to be a good place, really isn't—you'll never get
> away from trouble there. It would be very different, though,
> if you were to climb up on the Way and its Virtue and go
> drifting and wandering, neither praised nor damned, now a
> dragon, now a snake, shifting with the times, never willing
> to hold to one course only. Now up, now down, taking
> harmony for your measure, drifting and wandering with the
> ancestor of the ten thousand things, treating things as things
> but not letting them treat you as a thing—then how could
> you get into any trouble?[25] [60*a*]

[24] *Chuang-tzu* 19, tr. H. A. Giles (1), p. 232, mod. auct.
[25] *Chuang-tzu* 20, tr. Watson (1), pp. 209–10.

Later in the chapter he returns to the same theme:

> Mark what I say! In the case of the body, it is best to let
> it go along with things. In the case of the emotions, it is best
> to let them follow where they will. By going along with
> things, you avoid becoming separated from them. By letting
> the emotions follow as they will, you avoid fatigue.[26] [60*b*]

But it is worth re-emphasizing the principle that "you" cannot
go along with "things" unless there is the understanding that
there is, in truth, no alternative since you and the things are
the same process—the now-streaming Tao. The feeling that
there is a difference is also that process. There is nothing to
do about it. There is nothing not to do about it. There is only
the stream and its myriad convolutions—waves, bubbles,
spray, whirlpools, and eddies—and you *are* that.

One would like to leave it at that—except that such a statement evokes, in many minds, a tumult of questions. Instead
of experiencing the now-streaming—which would make everything clear—they want all kinds of preliminary guarantees
that it will be safe and profitable to do so, as to whether this
understanding "works" as a philosophy of life. Of course it
does, and very effectively, but if one follows it for that reason, one will not be following it. But if there is the understanding, the power or virtue of *te* arises spontaneously, or, as
Christians say, by divine grace as distinct from will-power. In
realizing that you are the Tao, you automatically manifest
its magic—but magic, as a grace, is something to which no
one should lay claim. As Lao-tzu says of the Tao itself, "When
good things are accomplished, it does not claim (or, name)
them."

[26] Ibid., p. 216.

善為士者不武善戰者不怒善勝
敵者不與善用人者為之下

[a: 108]

上仁為之而无以為上義為之而
有以為上禮為之而莫之應則攘
辟而扔之

[b: 109]

大道廢安有仁義智慧出安有大偽六
親不知有孝慈國家昏亂有貞臣

[c: 112]

五色令人目盲五音令人耳聾五
味令人口爽

[d: 120]

天下多忌諱而民彌貧民多利器
國家滋昏人多伎巧奇物滋起法
令滋彰盜賊多有 [b: 86]

徳為之而有以為

是以无德上德无為而无以為下 [c: 108]

上德不德是以有德下德不失德

大成若缺其用不弊大盈若沖其
用不窮大直若屈大巧若拙大辯
若訥 [d: 108]

100

天下莫柔弱於水而攻堅強者莫

之能勝

將欲取天下而為之吾見其不得

已天下神器不可為也為者敗之

執者失之 [b: 52]

道常無為而無不為 [c: 75]

小國寡民使有什伯之器而不用

使民重死而不遠徙雖有舟輿無

所乘之雖有甲兵無所陳之使人

復結繩而用之甘其食美其服安

其居樂其俗鄰國相望雞犬之聲

[a: 47]

101

重為輕根靜為躁君 [b: 41]

無名天地之始有名萬物之母故
常無欲以觀其妙常有欲以觀其
徼此兩者同出而異名同謂之玄
玄之又玄眾妙之門 [c: 44]

上善若水水善利萬物而不爭處
眾人之所惡故幾於道 [d: 47]

譬道之在天下猶川谷之於江海 [e: 47]

江海所以能為百谷王者以其善
下之故能為百谷王 [f: 47]

天下之至柔馳騁天下之至堅 [g: 47]

102

我無為而民自化 我好靜而民自正 我無事而民自富 我無欲而民自樸

[a: 32]

道生一 一生二 二生三 三生萬物

[b: 34]

道可道非常道

[c. 38]

大道泛兮其可左右 萬物恃之而生而不辭 功成不名有 衣養萬物而不為主

[d: 40]

有物混成先天地生 寂兮寥兮 獨立不改 周行而不殆 可以為天下母

41]

不出户知天下
知不證宇不牖為天下豁每 [a. 20]
狀常獸不靜 [b. 22]
天下皆知美之為美斯惡已皆知
善之為善斯不善已故有每相生
難易相成長短相較高下相傾音
声相和前後相隨 [c. 22]
三十輻共一毂當其無有車之用
埏埴以為器當其無有器之用鑿
户牖以為室當其無有室之用故
有之以為利無之以為用 [d. 23]

# NOTE

The calligraphy on pages 56–73 and 99–104 was written by Lee Chih-chang at the request of Alan Watts. It reproduces in Chinese the most important quotations from the early philosophers that appear in this book.

Although the calligraphic pages are numbered in the English order, from front to back, the calligraphy itself follows the Chinese order and reads from back to front, from right to left on the page, and vertically down the columns. The number that follows the identifying letter in brackets at the end of each quotation refers the reader to the page on which the English translation of that quotation can be found. For example, quotation *b* on facing page 104 appears in English translation on page 22, where it is identified by the number 104*b* in brackets.

Pages 56–73 contain mostly selections from the works of Chuang-tzu; pages 99–104, quotations from Lao-tzu. The arrangement of these passages on the calligraphic pages does not necessarily correspond to the order of their appearance in the English text.

# 5. Te—Virtuality

德

As it is said that the Tao as
described is not the real Tao, so one might
say that *te* (virtue or virtuality) as either contrived
or prescribed is not genuine *te*. Let us remind ourselves
that Taoism is based on the recognition that the world as

described is included in but is not the same as the world as it is. As a way of contemplation, it is being aware of life without thinking about it, and then carrying this on even while one is thinking, so that thoughts are not confused with nature. This sounds contradictory until one has experienced it, as by following the suggestions at the end of the second chapter.

*Te* is the realization or expression of the Tao in actual living, but this is not virtue in the sense of moral rectitude. It is rather as when we speak of the healing virtues of a plant, having the connotation of power or even magic, when magic refers to wonderful and felicitous events which come about spontaneously. In theistic terms, *te* is what happens "by the grace of God" as distinct from human striving, though without the implication of any supernatural intervention in the course of nature. We might call it "virtuality" as the word was used by William Caxton to mean the possession of force or power, or as when Sir Thomas Browne said that "in one graine of corne there lyeth dormant the virtuality of many other, and from thence sometimes proceed an hundred eares." *Te* is thus already present in the "miraculous" fruition of plants, the formation of eyes and ears, the circulation of blood, and the reticulation of nerves—since all this comes about without conscious direction. Cultures which limit the definition of "self" to the faculty of conscious attention therefore attribute these workings to an external God, or to "unconscious mechanisms" (*dei ex machina*).

But for the Taoists there is more to *te* than our ordinary natural functioning, even though "ordinary mind [*hsin*] is the  Tao." *Te* is also the unusual and thus remarkable naturalness of the sage—his unself-conscious and uncontrived skill in handling social and practical affairs, which John Lilly calls "coincidence control."

> Superior virtue [*te*] is not (intentionally) virtuous,
>     and thus is virtue.
> Inferior virtue does not let go of being virtuous,
>     and thus is not virtue.
> Superior virtue uses no force,
>     but nothing is left undone.
> Inferior virtue uses force,
>     but achieves nothing.[1] [100*c*]

But *te* often goes unnoticed because of its apparent ordinariness, as if it involved a sort of spiritual camouflage or anonymity like the unintentional protective coloring of a bird or moth.

> The greatest perfection seems imperfect;
> Yet its use will last without decay.
> The greatest fullness seems empty;
> Yet its use cannot be exhausted.
> The greatest straightness seems crooked;
> The greatest dexterity seems awkward;
> The greatest eloquence seems stammering.[2] [100*d*]

And so also:

> The best soldier is not soldierly;
> The best fighter is not ferocious;
> The best conqueror does not take part in war;
> The best employer of men keeps himself below them.[3]
> [99*a*]

This, however, is not deliberate self-effacement, not punishment of oneself, and not assumed humility in the presence of That which is greater than ourselves. It is more like the innocent practicality of a cat—though "knowing," in that the sage is well aware of the artificialities of the world of men.

One could say that *te* is natural virtue, based on inner feeling, as distinct from artificial virtue, based on a following of rules—but doesn't this raise an artificial distinction between

[1] *Lao-tzu* 38, tr. auct.
[2] *Lao-tzu* 45, tr. Ch'u Ta-kao (1), p. 60.
[3] *Lao-tzu* 68, tr. Ch'u Ta-kao (1), p. 83.

the natural and the artificial? Perhaps such a distinction does not exist fundamentally, since "the Tao is that from which nothing can deviate." But those who do not realize this try to harmonize themselves with the Tao by attempting to state the principles of nature in words, and then to follow them as if they were laws. So Lao-tzu continues his chapter on *te:*

> (Even) the best will in the world [*jen*], when forced,
> achieves nothing.
> The best righteousness, when forced,
> achieves nothing.
> The best good-form, when forced,
> does not come out right,
> and so, as ever, mere "elbow-grease" is used
> to enforce law.[4] [99*b*]

*Te* is thus the natural miracle of one who seems born to be wise and humane, comparable to what we call "perfect specimens" of flowers, trees, or butterflies—though sometimes our notions of the perfect specimen are too formal. Thus Chuang-tzu enlarges on the extraordinary virtue of being a hunchback, and goes on to suggest that being weird in mind may be even more advantageous than being weird in body. He compares the hunchback to a vast tree which has grown to a great old age by virtue of being useless for human purposes because its leaves are inedible and its branches twisted and pithy.[5] Formally healthy and upright humans are conscripted as soldiers, and straight and strong trees are cut down for lumber; wherefore the sage gets by with a perfect appearance of imperfection, such as we see in the gnarled pines and craggy hills of Chinese painting.

[4] *Lao-tzu* 38, tr. auct. This chapter is translated in so many ways that it is sometimes hard to realize that they represent the same Chinese text. I have had to assume, for the sake of consistency, that in the second sentence (on righteousness) *yu* should be read as *wu*.

[5] See *Chuang-tzu* 4, where he also notes that such trees are regarded as sacred.

Many passages in Taoist literature illustrate *te* in terms of various skills—of the carpenter, butcher, wheelwright, boatman, and so forth.

> Ch'ui the artisan could draw circles with his hand better than with compasses. His fingers seemed to accommodate themselves so naturally to the thing he was working at, that it was unnecessary to fix his attention. His mental faculties thus remained one, and suffered no hindrance.[6] [66a]

> Those who cannot make perfect without arc, line, compasses, and square, injure the natural constitution of things. Those who require cords to bind and glue to stick, interfere with the natural functions of things. And those who seek to satisfy the mind of man by fussing with ceremonies and music and preaching charity and duty to one's neighbor, thereby destroy the intrinsic nature of things. For there is such an intrinsic nature in things, in this sense:—Things which are curved require no arcs; things which are straight require no lines; things which are round require no compasses; things which are rectangular require no squares; things which stick require no glue; things which hold together require no cords.[7] [57a]

In this way old-fashioned Japanese carpenters use no blueprints and judge everything by eye, putting together marvelous pieces of joinery without nails or glue. But the art is being lost because their children, who should begin studying the craft at least by the time they are seven years old, must instead be sent to school to learn bureaucracy and business.

> Ch'ing, the chief carpenter, was carving wood into a stand for hanging musical instruments. When finished, the work appeared to those who saw it as though of supernatural execution. And the prince of Lu asked him, saying, "What mystery is there in your art?"
>
> "No mystery, your Highness," replied Ch'ing; "and yet there is something. When I am about to make such a stand, I guard against any diminution of my vital power. I first reduce my mind to absolute quiescence. Three days in this

[6] *Chuang-tzu* 19, tr. H. A. Giles (1), p. 242.
[7] *Chuang-tzu* 8, tr. H. A. Giles (1), pp. 101–2, mod. auct.

condition, and I become oblivious of any reward to be gained. Five days, and I become oblivious of any fame to be acquired. Seven days, and I become unconscious of my four limbs and my physical frame. Then, with no thought of the Court present in my mind, my skill becomes concentrated, and all disturbing elements from without are gone. I enter some mountain forest. I search for a suitable tree. It contains the form required, which is afterwards elaborated. I see the stand in my mind's eye, and then set to work. Otherwise, there is nothing. I bring my own natural capacity into relation with that of the wood. What was suspected to be of supernatural execution in my work was due solely to this."[8] [65a]

Remembering that Chuang-tzu puts his own words into the mouth of Confucius, there is this about the skill of the boatman:

Yen Yüan said to Confucius, "When I crossed over the Shang-shen rapid, the boatman managed his craft with marvellous skill. I asked him if handling a boat could be learnt. 'It can,' replied he. 'The way of those who know how to keep you afloat is more like sinking you. They row as if the boat wasn't there.' I enquired what this meant, but he would not tell me. May I ask its signification?"

"It means," answered Confucius, "that such a man is oblivious of the water around him. He regards the rapid as though dry land. He looks upon an upset as an ordinary cart accident. And if a man can but be impervious to capsizings and accidents in general, whither should he not be able comfortably to go?"[9] [66b]

But the expert cannot always explain the secret of his craft, and even when, in the Chuang-tzu writings, he does explain, the explanation is always somewhat elusive. Here is the wheelwright speaking:

[8] *Chuang-tzu* 19, tr. H. A. Giles (1), pp. 240–41.
[9] *Chuang-tzu* 19, tr. H. A. Giles (1), pp. 233–34. But there is a very different rendering in Watson (1), p. 200, where the boatman says, "Certainly. A good swimmer will in no time get the knack of it. And if a man can swim under water, he may never have seen a boat before and still he'll know how to handle it!"

> In making a wheel, if you work too slowly, you can't make it firm; if you work too fast, the spokes won't fit in. You must go neither too slowly nor too fast. There must be co-ordination of mind and hand. Words cannot explain what it is, but there is some mysterious art herein. I cannot teach it to my son; nor can he learn it from me. Consequently, though seventy years of age, I am still making wheels in my old age.[10] [59b]

But there is the irresistible temptation in us to find out *how,* which is to learn the secret by a linear, step-by-step method, or to be told in words. How is it that people ask for, say, dancing to be explained to them, instead of just watching and following? Why is there formal instruction to teach something so natural as swimming? Why do human beings have to read books to understand copulation? The mythologies of many cultures contain, in varying ways, the theme that man has fallen from grace and has had to replace it with technology.

> When the great Tao was lost,
> there came (ideas of) humanity and justice.
> When knowledge and cleverness arrived,
> there came great deceptions.
> When familial relations went out of harmony,
> there came (ideas of) good parents and loyal children.
> When the nation fell into disorder and misrule,
> there came (ideas of) loyal ministers.[11] [99c]

The organization of the physical organism is far more complex than that of any political or commercial corporation, and yet it works with a minimum of conscious control. The circuits of brain and nerve are more subtle than any computer system, and we hardly know how we grew them. But when history began we put on clothes, picked up tools, and learned how to speak and think. In the words of Lancelot Whyte:

> Thought is born of failure. When action satisfies there is no residue to hold the attention; to think is to confess a

[10] *Chuang-tzu* 13, tr. H. A. Giles (1), p. 171.
[11] *Lao-tzu* 18, tr. auct.

lack of adjustment which we must stop to consider. Only when the human organism fails to achieve an adequate response to its situation is there material for the processes of thought, and the greater the failure the more searching they become. . . . Confucius is the first clear example of a man in this situation. Concerned at the disintegration of primitive Chinese civilization, he sought to restore order by relying on the power of ideas to organize behavior. He was aware of what he was trying to do: society was to be set right by calling everything by its right name, or as he put it, by the "rectification of names" [*cheng ming*].[12]

正名

The Taoists saw the "rectification of names" as a vicious circle, for with what names are the right names to be defined? The conscious control of life seems to involve us in ever more bewildering webs of complexity so that, despite their initial successes, technics create more problems than they solve.

The failure from which thought is born is, of course, failure to survive. The Contemplative Taoists, while rejecting the quest for immortality, were certainly concerned with "living out one's natural term of life," which is why Chuang-tzu commended the hunchback and the useless tree. But they are also saying that the chances of survival are best when there is no anxiety to survive, and that the greatest power (*te*) is available to those who do not seek power and who do not use force. To be anxious to survive is to wear oneself out, and to seek power and use force is to overstrain one's system. One is best preserved by floating along without stress, all of which is the same as Jesus' doctrine of not being anxious for the morrow, and the *Bhagavad-Gita*'s principle of action without concern for results (*nishkama karma*). This theme runs throughout the spiritual literature of the world: that you will get it if you do not want (i.e., lack) it, and that to him that hath shall be given.

To those who feel that they have not, this is an exasperating paradox. If, deep down inside, you want most desperately to

12 Whyte (1), p. 1.

survive and to be in control of things, you cannot genuinely take the attitude of not worrying about it. Yet, surely, trying to stop the worry is still effort to control, and, in the spirit of *wu-wei,* you must allow yourself the freedom to worry—to "let the mind think whatever it wants to think" (Lieh-tzu). But "you must allow yourself" is just a way of talking, a grammatic fiction, since—to drive the point home—you are at least all that you experience, and your mind or consciousness is identical with what we call space, all of it. If someone cuts off your head, this, and all the terror involved, is what you are doing to yourself. The total unconsciousness which "follows" is the intense negative counterpart of the intense positive sensation of being alive and real, the *yin* aspect of the *yang.* The prospect, *and memory,* of very real death—total annihilation—are what give verve and importance to life. As in the *yin-yang* symbol of the double helix, they are the alternating pulses of that eternal series of surprises called oneself, in which the forgettory is as necessary as the memory. Thus Chuang-tzu writes of the death of Lao-tzu:

> The Master came because it was time. He left because he followed the natural flow. Be content with the moment, and be willing to follow the flow; then there will be no room for grief or joy. In the old days this was called freedom from bondage. The wood is consumed but the fire burns on, and we do not know when it will come to an end.[13] [61a]

Hsien Taoism, with its yogic and alchemical practices for attaining immortality or, at least, great longevity, was therefore almost the antithesis of the Lao-tzu and Chuang-tzu teachings. Such practices must have existed already in Chuang-tzu's time, for he ridicules them:

> To exhale and inhale, to puff out old breath and draw in new, to stretch like a bear and crane like a bird, with concern only for longevity—all this is induced Tao [*tao-yin*],

[13] *Chuang-tzu* 3 ad fin., tr. Gia-fu Feng (2), p. 59.

practiced by hygienists who hope to live as long as P'eng Tsu.[14] [57b]

Somewhat comparable is the difference in Buddhism between the Way of Wisdom (*prajna*) and the Way of Powers (*siddhi*). Intuitive understanding may or may not give one supernormal powers which function to the extent that they are not forcefully willed or claimed, for the truly awakened ones know that their real *siddhi* is everything going on in the universe. On the other hand, *siddhi,* such as telepathy and clairvoyance, may be cultivated by special disciplines just as exercises are used for physical hygiene. But however far such disciplines may be pursued they do not lead to *prajna,* but tend rather to obstruct it by encouraging the sort of ego-centricity which is often noted in great athletes and actors. Thus Chuang-tzu reproves Po Lo for his excessive skill in training horses:

> Horses live on dry land, eat grass and drink water. When pleased, they rub their necks together. When angry, they turn round and kick up their heels at each other. Thus far only do their natural dispositions carry them. But bridled and bitted, with a plate of metal on their foreheads, they learn to cast vicious looks, to turn the head to bite, to resist, to get the bit out of the mouth or the bridle into it. And thus their natures become depraved—the fault of Po Lo.[15] * [64a]

[14] *Chuang-tzu* 15, tr. auct., adjuv. H. A. Giles (1) and Watson (1). The term *tao-yin* refers to breathing exercises comparable to *pranayama* in Yoga. P'eng Tsu is the Chinese counterpart of Methuselah. However, in *Chuang-tzu* 6 it is said that "the pure men of old drew breath from their uttermost depths; the vulgar only from their throats." The point, as I see it, is that if the breath is allowed to follow its own course it will of itself become slow and deep, so that there is no need for artificial exercises. Cf. Welch (1), pp. 92–93.

[15] *Chuang-tzu* 9, tr. H. A. Giles (1), pp. 108–9. Presumably this is the source from which the game of polo gets its name.

* Also, the Chinese character 偽 , meaning "false," "simulated," or "counterfeit," can be literally translated as what man 人 does to horses 馬 . Pictorially, the character *wei*, as in *wu-wei*, looks like a horse being tamed and manipulated by man. See Chapter 4, "*Wu-wei*," above, pp. 74–98.

To blend the Taoist and Buddhist terms, we might say that *te* is the virtuality, the grace in living, which comes naturally from *prajna*—the intuitive realization of being one with the Tao. *Te* is not to be confused with *siddhi* as cultivated by psychophysical gymnastics. However, the following passage from Chuang-tzu is often cited by Hsien Taoists as authority for the cultivation of miraculous powers:

> He who understands the Way [Tao] is certain to have command of basic principles. He who has command of basic principles is certain to know how to deal with circumstances. And he who knows how to deal with circumstances will not allow things to do him harm. When a man has perfect virtue [*te*], fire cannot burn him, water cannot drown him, cold and heat cannot afflict him, birds and beasts cannot injure him.

But, he goes on to say:

> I do not say that he makes light of these things. I mean that he distinguishes between safety and danger, contents himself with fortune or misfortune, and is cautious in his comings and goings. Therefore nothing can harm him.[16] [58b]

In other words, his freedom from harm is due, not to magic, but to intelligent circumspection.

楊朱

Lieh-tzu, although having the reputation of being able to ride on the wind,[17] quotes Yang Chu—with apparent approval—in a passage which seems to go even further than Chuang-tzu in praise of taking life easily:

> Let the ear hear what it longs to hear, the eye see what it longs to see, the nose smell what it likes to smell, the mouth speak what it wants to speak, let the body have every comfort that it craves, let the mind do as it will. Now what the ear wants to hear is music, and to deprive it of this is

[16] *Chuang-tzu* 17, tr. Watson (1), p. 182.

[17] As already suggested, I doubt if this is to be taken literally. To ride the wind must be an equivalent of what we call walking on air or being lighthearted.

to cramp the sense of hearing. What the eye wants to see is carnal beauty; and to deprive it is to cramp the sense of sight. What the nose craves for is to have near it the fragrant plants *shu* [dogwood] and *lan* [orchids]; and if it cannot have them, the sense of smell is cramped. What the mouth desires is to speak of what is true and what false; and if it may not speak, then knowledge is cramped. What the body desires for its comfort is warmth and good food. Thwart its attainment of these, and you cramp what is natural and essential to man. What the mind wants is liberty to stray whither it will, and if it has not this freedom, the very nature of man is cramped and thwarted. Tyrants and oppressors cramp us in every one of these ways. Let us depose them, and wait happily for death to come.[18]

But this passage might easily be misunderstood if not read in conjunction with Chuang-tzu's idea of "fasting the heart (mind)" (*hsin chai*). The words are again put into the mouth of Confucius, speaking to one who has practiced ordinary, or religious, fasting to no effect.

You are trying to unify yourself, so you don't listen with your ears but with your heart (mind); you don't listen with your mind but with your spirit [*ch'i*].★ (Let) hearing stop with the ears, and the mind stop at thinking (or, at symbols). Then the spirit is a void embracing everything, and only the Tao includes the void. This void is the fasting of the heart (mind).[19] [61*b*]

[18] *Lieh-tzu* 7.5, tr. Waley (1), pp. 41–42.

[19] *Chuang-tzu* 4, tr. auct. The text here is ambiguous. Fung Yu-lan, Lin Yutang, and Watson take the words up to the ★ to be in the imperative, whereas Giles reads them in the indicative, which seems to me correct. To say, "Do not listen with your ears, but with your mind" (imperative) does not go along with the metaphor of fasting the mind. Pure linguistics doesn't help much here, for one has to understand the passage in the light of Chuang-tzu's philosophy as a whole. A much later text, the *T'ai I Chin Hua Tsung Chih* (a +17th-century rendition of a T'ang tradition), says: "When a person looks at something, listens to something, eyes and ears move and follow the things until they have passed. These movements are all underlings, and when the Heavenly ruler [i.e., the *ch'i*] follows them in their tasks, it means: To live together with demons" (tr. Wilhelm [2], p. 61). This seems to catch the sense of this "fasting" as explained below.

To understand this we must go back to the basic Taoist philosophy of natural order and political government. "The Tao loves and nourishes all things, but does not lord it over them." So, in the same way, the government of the body and psyche must not be egocentric. The senses, feelings, and thoughts must be allowed to be spontaneous (*tzu-jan*) in the faith that they will then order themselves harmoniously. To try to control the mind forcefully is like trying to flatten out waves with a board, and can only result in more and more disturbance. As some of our own psychotherapists have put it, "Leave your mind alone"—and this is surely what Chuang-tzu means by fasting it. Thus "trying to unify yourself" must mean trying to subject your organism to autocratic government. There is a clear parallel in the psychology of Indian Yoga, as when it is said in the *Gita:*

> The man who is united with the Divine and knows the truth thinks "I do nothing at all" for in seeing, hearing, touching, smelling, tasting, walking, sleeping, breathing; in speaking emitting, grasping, opening and closing the eyes he holds that only the senses are occupied with the objects of the senses.[20]

In many cultures people are brought up to mistrust their own organisms, and, as children, are taught to control their thoughts, emotions, and appetites by muscular efforts such as clenching the teeth or fists, frowning to concentrate attention, scratching the head to think, staring to see, holding the breath or tightening the diaphragm or rectum to inhibit emotion. These strainings are largely futile because the nervous system is not muscle but electric circuitry, and one does not use a sledge hammer for tuning a radio. Those who raise children in this way are simply unintelligent people who think that mere force can achieve anything. They remind one of the

[20] *Bhagavad-Gita* 5. 8–9, tr. Radhakrishnan (1), p. 177.

story of a cigar-chewing Texan who harnessed a kitten to his broken-down Cadillac. When bystanders pointed out that this was absurd, he replied, "You-all may think so, but I got a horsewhip."

The human organism has the same kind of innate intelligence as the ecosystems of nature, and the wisdom of the nerves and senses must be watched with patience and respect. This is why, as Joseph Needham points out, the Taoists contributed far more to Chinese science than the Confucians, for whereas the latter had their noses in books and were concerned with the following of rules, the former were observers of nature. Taoist literature abounds with comments on the behavior of animals, insects, reptiles, plants, wind, water, and the heavenly bodies, whereas Confucian literature is almost exclusively preoccupied with political and social relations. He goes on to show, with parallels from the West, that mysticism and empiricism go together in opposition to scholasticism— that they base themselves on the nonlinear world of experience rather than the linear world of letters. What is important for the mystic is not belief in the right doctrine but attainment of the true experience, whereas the scholastic theologians would not look through Galileo's telescope because they considered that they already knew, from Scripture, the order of the heavens. The scientist and the mystic both make experiments in which what has been written is always subordinate to the observation of what is.[21]

Confucians, along with Hebrew, Islamic, and Catholic scholastics, as well as Protestant fundamentalists, are like tourists

[21] Needham (1), vol. 2, pp. 89–98. It should also be pointed out that the mysticism of the Brothers of the Free Spirit, the Anabaptists, the Levellers, and the Quakers underlies the political philosophy of Jefferson and others who formulated the sadly neglected Constitution of the United States. As I have suggested elsewhere, there is a peculiar contradiction in trying to be the loyal citizen of a republic while believing that the universe is a monarchy.

who study guidebooks and maps instead of wandering freely and looking at the view. Speech and writing are undoubtedly marvelous, but for this very reason they have a hypnotic and fascinating quality which can lead to the neglect of nature itself until they become too much of a good thing. Thus when "the rule of law" becomes absolutized and everything is done by the book or the computer, people call out in desperation for the intervention of a reasonable human being.

This is why there are no rules for *te,* and why there can be no textbook for instructing judges and lawyers in the senses of equity and fair play. One has to have the "feel" for it, in the same way that Chuang-tzu's wheelwright had the feel for making wheels but could not put it into words. The same is true in music, painting, and cookery, for Lao-tzu says:

> The five colors blind one's eyes;
> The five tones deafen one's ears;
> The five tastes ruin one's palate.[22] [99*d*]

He is, of course, referring to the formal rules and classifications for these arts, as to say that if you think there are only five colors, you must be blind, and deaf if you think that all music has to be in the pentatonic scale. This is, alas, the reason why schools for these various arts produce so few geniuses, and why the genius—the person of *te*—is always going beyond the rules, not because of an obstreperous and antisocial spirit with hostile intent, but because the fountain of creative work is an intelligent questioning of the rules. The early Taoists were therefore questioning the validity of normal Chinese, and generally Confucian, common sense.

Thus, in the modern West as also in Communist China and industrial Japan, the Taoist would be asking awkward questions concerning basic assumptions about the good life. Is it

---

[22] *Lao-tzu* 12, tr. auct.

so good a thing to go on living for a long time? Would you rather go off with a prolonged whimper or with a glorious bang? Would you really like to hold a position of power, such as the presidency of the United States or of a great corporation, wherein you must make momentous decisions at almost every moment and never be separated from the telephone? And how about becoming so famous that you are recognized wherever you go, and so rich that everyone wants to rob you? Or what is so good about a country of organized mediocrity, in which everyone must eat the same, dress the same, and dwell the same—since everyone knows that variety is the spice of life?

At root, then, the idea of *te* is power exercised without the use of force and without undue interference with the order of surrounding circumstances.

> Entering the forest without moving the grass;
> Entering the water without raising a ripple.[23]

Going back to the original form of the ideogram, *te* means going along with unity of eye and heart (mind). This is intelligent perception of the course of things, as the navigator observes the stars and the sailor watches the currents and winds. Thor Heyerdahl's (1) story *Kon-Tiki* is a perfect example of *te* in operation, showing how he and his crew drifted on a balsa-wood raft from Peru to distant islands in the South Seas just by going along with the natural processes of the ocean. Yet this intelligence is more than mere calculation and measurement. It includes that; but Heyerdahl's genius was that he had a basic trust in the unified system of his own organism and the ecosystem of the Pacific, and was therefore almost as intelligent as a dolphin. By virtue of this attitude he was helped along by events which he had not consciously expected.

[23] *Zenrin Kushu* 10, p. 164, tr. auct.

In water, the balsa wood swelled so as to bind the logs of the raft more securely, and almost every morning there were flying-fish on the deck for breakfast.

In a material and practical sense, Heyerdahl and such other Taoists succeed. But their success depends on a confidence and lack of self-frustrating anxiety which in turn is derived from the insight that in the course of nature, and in following the line of least resistance, nothing can go wrong. I do not think this is the superficial attitude of Pangloss, of the hearty and thoughtless view that this is the best of all possible worlds.

However, to say that it is much more difficult and subtle than that will dismay simplehearted people and delight those proud intellectual athletes who need to be quite sure that, in attaining wisdom, they have done something extremely arduous. The superficiality of Voltaire's Pangloss is that he is all talk, and will not willingly and shamelessly scream when eaten by a shark. Certainly he will scream, but he will feel that in so doing he has betrayed his philosophy—not realizing that screaming and squirming are the natural way of going along with pain. Taoism is not a philosophy of compelling oneself to be calm and dignified under all circumstances. The real and astonishing calm of people like Lao-tzu comes from the fact that they are ready and willing, without shame, to do whatever comes naturally in all circumstances. The unbelievable result is that they are far more sociable and civilized than those who try to live rigorously by laws and watchwords.

# Once Again: A New Beginning

Al Chung-liang Huang

FIVE YEARS AGO when my father was dying, my wife and I were most grateful to know that another life very dear to us was growing inside her body. Our second child was conceived shortly after Alan's passing. During my early months of mourning for him, I was happy to realize that a new life would continue to contain and radiate the energy and spirit of the Tao.

On August 20, 1974, nine months after Alan's departure, long enough for a ripened fruition, I began to write these pages during labor and delivery with my wife, Suzanne. I was almost certain that this, indeed, was what Alan had meant by "fun and surprises."

While breathing to ride the waves of each of Suzanne's

accelerated contractions, we began to rediscover the meaning of "labor." "Woman in labor." What a strange expression to describe such spontaneous muscular activity of the uterus when it is ready to expel the full-grown fetus! On the other hand, the word "labor" can be perfectly neutral when applied to nonintellectuals. Primitive people work naturally in hunting and fishing. Farmers labor to till the land. Peasant women labor easily during childbirth, often while still working in the fields. Only we, the intellectuals, find the concept of labor misleading.

[My father came from a strict Confucian upbringing. He would never have entertained the notion of witnessing the birth of any one of his seven children, although my mother had always had the choice and dignity of having her children in her own bed. Only once, during the war, was she forced to subject herself to the antiseptic bureaucracy of a hospital. Even then, with all the medical staff gone because of heavy bombing, my grandmother delivered me, relying simply on her instinctive female knowhow.]

When my first daughter, Lark, was born, I shared with Alan my revelation and joy. I had experienced as closely as I was able the process of giving birth and being born. I was ecstatic and danced all night long in the moonlight afterwards. I became keenly aware of the superficiality and egocentricity in all my various artistic endeavors. It was clear to me that no matter how I strove I could never surpass that transcendental experience. Alan was delighted and confessed to me his initial reluctance and resistance to such an adventure until the birth of one of his grandchildren. Like me, he had realized that all his years of reading and writing about cosmic union, sexual entity, and universal nature could not measure up to that one real experience. It was truly a miracle to see and feel the happening of the small universe contained in the human infant.

We reminded each other of all the Taoist stories of craftsmen-artisans who told about the impossibility of transmitting their arts to future generations. True knowledge can be encompassed only by instinct and by actual experience. How sad and ludicrous to admit that we must go to classes to learn how to breathe properly and take lessons in such natural skills as swimming, dancing, and making love.

For a long time old friends remembered Alan Watts as the brilliant young scholar, stiff, proper, and basically very shy. During his life he went through many changes, becoming transformed from the slightly stuffy, slightly snobbish personality with the old-country upbringing, so that by the time I first knew him he was identified mostly by his role as guru to the flower children. He was criticized by his peers, especially the academicians, for what appeared to them this abrupt full swing to the other side. They were envious of him, also, because he was obviously having a wonderful time.

Through his theatrical talents and game-plays, Alan was able to forgo many of his Victorian inhibitions and create for himself and others a curious kind of balance which somehow sustained him. In later life, he depended more on his external need to perform and to receive support from his audience. Constantly pulled by outside demands, he was too successful to stop—and too brilliant to submit to his own nature. He became the perfect example of the Western man as victim of the *yang*-dominant world. He revealed the crux of this tragedy shared by most men in this unbalanced time by admitting, "But I don't like myself when I am sober," as he surrendered to another shot of vodka at a time when he knew he need not and should not rely on it any more.

When I first came to America I was amazed to find how

hard it was for people to touch one another, and to see the reluctance of men to share simple affection. Alan was no exception. We liked each other right away, but the few times I remember his being affectionate and embraceable were usually after we had been dancing. And in order to dance as easily and joyously as we did, a few loosening-up drinks were often necessary. I could always sense the strain in Alan and feel his constant struggle to transcend his heavy intellectual burdens. Alan's journey to his own East had not been an easy one, for he was the kind of man who created traps for himself with his own words and then had to maneuver his way in and out of them. On the last page of his autobiography, *In My Own Way,* he wrote: "I have tried for years, as a philosopher, but in words it comes out all wrong: in black and white with no color. . . . when you try to pin [life] down you get the banality of formal nihilism, wherein the universe is seen as 'a tale told by an idiot, full of sound and fury, signifying nothing.' But this sense of 'turning to ashes in one's mouth' is the result of trying to grasp something which can only come to you of itself." Was he at the threshold of giving up that "grasping," and had that "something" begun coming to him of itself?

I met Alan Watts after a year's visit with my father at home in China, having already spent fourteen years in America. Back in California, I was totally disoriented in my multiple identities. I was treading precariously on the two shores of my personal cultural split. Alan reconfirmed my belief that the East-West balance had always existed within myself, as a personal growing experience. I recognized in Alan a rare and wonderful ability to be both Occidental and Oriental. When he allowed it, he could be both at once, easily bridging the gaps within his own learning and experience. Unlike so many Westerners who try to be Oriental by disinheriting their own culture, Alan could be simply himself. He knew that a blue-eyed, pink-skinned guru could be just as inscrutable as a slitty-eyed, yellow-skinned one. There was no reason for him to be foreign to either the West or the East. He reminded us by his own successes as well as failures how perfectly natural life's imbalance is to all of us. He showed us how Eastern philosophy has been gradually permeating all walks of life in the West while everyone laments the disappearance of the gentle East under increasing technological and industrial demands. Undoubtedly, there will be more freeways and polluting chimneys in the East while most great masters of the Orient are emigrating one by one to the mountains and growth-center retreats in the West. I often prepare my friends and students for the shock of discovering the next Chinese they meet to be well versed in technological jargon but completely ignorant of *t'ai chi* or Tao. The majority of friends of kindred spirit who have shared my studies of the East have been Westerners.

An old Chinese parable tells how the two fastest horses began a race with the sun behind them in the *east* and at the end inevitably found themselves facing the sun in the *west*. Hermann Hesse's *Journey to the East* and Wu Ch'eng-en's *Journey to the West* (or *Monkey King*) share essentially the same theme. What is East and what is West? How can two words like *Tao* and *Dow* become an easy pun and paradox when they have the same sound yet are so different in essence? In Chinese, *East-West*, as a connecting two-word expression, means "a thing," "a something"—and perhaps "nothing" at all.

東
西

THE CHINESE CHARACTERS that appear on the cover and throughout this book have been executed in the spirit of the Tao. After each intellectual session on the existing chapters, I would prepare ink and brush and meditate on the essence of Alan's words and thoughts in Chinese, allowing them to move with me bodily until they were no longer separate from the dance. Still dancing, I would then roll out the rice paper and let it happen, moving the ink-filled brush continuously without stopping to think.

The Watercourse Way is not one man's way. It is the universal way. The calligraphy done by me is not really mine exclusively; it is also Alan Watts's, for so much of his spirit-energy had been embodied within me when I wrote these cursive words. It is yours too, our reader, when you are in tune with us in this watercourse way.

In essence, if you quickly leaf through the length of this book, simply following the connective energy from one calligraphic page to the next, you should be able to feel the spirit of the Tao. The words are thoughts for enjoyment, and you have here the words of the supreme master Alan himself to entertain you. Meanwhile, he is alerting you not to dwell upon the words; he wishes you to play and dance with these Chinese characters whenever you find your head heavy, your thoughts stuck.

The Tao is all here, in black or in white and in the in-between. After all, it was Alan who used to say, "When you get the message, hang up the phone!" So, enjoy your conversations with him; let the chatter-in-the-skull cease when your heart-minds are met. Put the book aside and dance for a while.

# Bibliography

## 1. Original Chinese Sources

CHIEH TZU YÜAN HUA CHUAN. 芥子園畫譜
The Mustard-Seed Garden Manual of Painting:
Classified Collections of Facsimiles of Chinese Old Masters.
Copies and Commentaries by Wang An-chieh and Lee Li-oon.
The Wen-kwang Book Store, Hong Kong, 1956.

CHU TZU K'AO SHIH. 諸子考釋
By Liang Ch'i-ch'ao (1873–1929).
Chung-hua Book Co., Taipei, 1957.

CHUANG-TZU. 莊子

(1) *Chuang-tzu Nan Hua Ching*.
Hsiang Ch'i Lao Jen, ed.
Chung-hua Book Co., Taipei, 1917.
Reprint, Hung-yeh Book Co., Taipei, 1969.

(2) *Chuang-tzu*.
Yeh Yu-lin, ed.
Kwang-yi Book Co., Shanghai, 1941.

(3) *Pai Hua Chuang-tzu Peng*.
Yeh Yu-lin, ed.
Wen-yuen Book Co., Taipei, 1967.

(4) *Chuang-tzu Yin Te*.
Harvard-Yenching Institute, Sinological Index Series No. 20, 1965.

CHUNG KUO CHE HSUEH SHIH. 中國哲學史
The History of Chinese Philosophy.
By Fung Yu-lan.
Commercial Press, Shanghai, 1934.

CHUNG KUO CHUNG KU SHIH
HSIANG CH'ANG PIEN. 中國中古思想長編
The Longhand Edition of Medieval Chinese Thoughts.
By Hu Shih.
The Hu Shih Memorial Series.
Mei-ya Publishers, Taipei, 1971.

129

## BIBLIOGRAPHY

CHUNG KUO KU TAI CHE HSUEH SHIH. 中國古代哲
The History of Ancient Chinese Philosophy. 學史
By Hu Shih.
Commercial Press, Shanghai, 1920.

HAN FEI TZU. 韓非子
Writings of Han Fei.
Wang Hsian-shen, ed.
Commercial Press, Taipei, 1965.

HSIEN CH'IN CHENG CHIH SSU 先秦政治思想史
HSIANG SHIH.
A History of China's Political Thoughts in the Pre-Ch'in Period.
By Liang Ch'i-ch'ao.
Commercial Press, Shanghai, 1925.

HUAI NAN TZU. 淮南子
Writings of Liu An, d. −122.
Kao Yu, ed. (+205–212).
Chung-hua Book Co., Taipei, 1966.

I CHING. 易經
The Book of Changes.
(1) *Han Shih Ching Chou I Ts'an Tsu Chi Cheng.*
    The Han Dynasty Stone Rubbing of *I Ching.*
    Ch'u Wan-li, ed.
    Historical Language Studies, Central Research Study Bureau
    Edition No. 46, Taipei, 1961.
(2) *I Ching Yun Ta I.*
    Hsieh Meng, ed., Yuan Dynasty.
    Commercial Press, Taipei, 1971.

KUAN-TZU. 管子
Writings of Kuan Chung, d. −122.
(1) Fang Hsuan-ling, ed., T'ang Dynasty, +578–648.
    Reprint, Cheh-chiang Book Co., 1876.
(2) T'ang Ching-kao, ed.
    Commercial Press, Shanghai, 1926; Commercial Press, Taipei,
    1967.

LAO-TZU: TAO TE CHING. 老子道德經
Original commentaries by Wang Pi, Wei Dynasty (+226–249).

*Chi T'ang Tzu Lao-tzu Tao Te Ching Chu.*
Reprint of *Ku I Ch'un Hsu Peng,* 1884.
I-wen Press, Taipei, 1950.

LI CHI. 禮記
Records of Rites.
Original commentaries by Cheng Hsuan, Han Dynasty.
(1) Harvard-Yenching Institute, Sinological Index Series No. 27.
Chinese Materials and Research Aids Service Center, Inc.,
Taipei, 1966.
(2) *Li Chi Chi Shieh.*
Sun Hsi-tan, ed.
Commercial Press, Taipei, 1965.
(3) *Li Chi Ching Hua Lu.*
Chung-hua Book Co., Taipei, 1966.

LIEH-TZU. 列子
Writings of Lieh Yu-ko, —4th century.
(1) Chang Kan, ed.
Commercial Press, Shanghai, 1959.
(2) T'ang Ching-kao, ed.
Commercial Press, Taipei, 1965.

SHIH CHI. 史記
Records of the Grand Historian of China.
By Ssu-ma Ch'ien.
Preface dated 1747.
Pei Yin, ed.
Tung-wen Book Co., Shanghai, 1884.
Later editions:  Ch'uin Hsueh Book Co., Shanghai, 1929.
Commercial Press, Shanghai, 1934.
Commercial Press, Taipei, 1965.
Chung-hua Book Co., Peking, 1973.

TAO CHIA SHIH TZU HSING PIEN. 道家四子新編
Taoism: Sacred Books.
By Yen Ling-feng.
Commercial Press, Taipei, 1968.

WU CH'IU PEI TSAI LAO-TZU CHI 無求備齋老子集
CH'ENG CHU PIEN. 成諸編
By Yen Ling-feng.
Chung-hua Book Co., Taipei, 1965.

BIBLIOGRAPHY

## 2. WORKS IN EUROPEAN LANGUAGES

Blofeld, John, ed. *The Zen Teaching of Huang Po on the Transmission of Mind*. Grove Press, New York, and Rider & Co., London, 1958.

Brown, G. Spencer. *Laws of Form*. George Allen & Unwin, London, 1969. Julian Press, New York, 1972.

Chan, Wing-tsit, tr. *The Platform Scripture of the Sixth Patriarch*. St. Johns University Press, Jamaica, N.Y., 1963.

Chiang, Yee. *Chinese Calligraphy*. Methuen & Co., London, 1938. 3rd ed., revised and enlarged, Harvard University Press, Cambridge, Mass., 1973.

Ch'u Ta-kao, tr. *Tao Te Ching* George Allen & Unwin for Buddhist Society, London, 1937.

Creel, Herrlee G. *What Is Taoism? and Other Studies in Chinese Cultural History*. University of Chicago Press, 1970.

Dhiegh, Khigh Alx. *The Eleventh Wing: An Exposition of the Dynamics of I Ching for Now*. Dell Publishing Co., New York, 1973.

Duthuit, Georges. *Chinese Mysticism and Modern Painting*. Chroniques du Jour, Paris, and A. Zwemmer, London, 1936.

Duyvendak, J. J. L., tr. *Tao Te Ching: The Book of the Way and Its Virtue*. John Murray, London, and Transatlantic Arts, Hollywood, Fla., 1954.

Feng, Gia-fu, and Jane English, trs. (1) *Tao Te Ching*. Alfred A. Knopf, New York, 1972. Wildwood House, London, 1973.
(2) *Chuang Tsu: Inner Chapters*. Alfred A. Knopf, New York, 1974.

Forke, Alfred. *The World-Conception of the Chinese*. Arthur Probsthain & Co., London, 1925.

Forrest, Robert Andrew. *The Chinese Language*. 2nd rev. ed. Humanities Press, New York, and Faber & Faber, London, 1965.

Fung Yu-lan (1) *A History of Chinese Philosophy*. 2 vols. Tr. Derk Bodde. Princeton University Press, and George Allen & Unwin, London, 1952–53.
(2) *A Short History of Chinese Philosophy*. Ed. Derk Bodde.
Free Press, New York, 1966.
(3) *Chuang Tzu: A New Selected Translation*. The Commercial Press, Shanghai, 1933. Repr., Paragon Book Reprint Corp., New York, 1963.

Gernet, J. "Entretiens du Maître de Dhyana Chen-houei du Ho-tsö." *Publications de l'École Française d'Extrême-Orient*, vol. 31. 1949.

Giles, Herbert A., tr. *Chuang Tzu: Mystic, Moralist, and Social Reformer*. Kelly & Walsh, Shanghai, 1926. Repr. AMS Press, New York, 1972.

Giles, Lionel, tr. *Taoist Teachings: From the Book of Lieh Tzu*. E. P.

Dutton, New York, and John Murray, London, 1912. Repr., Paragon Book Reprint Corp., New York, n.d.

Graham, Angus Charles. *Two Chinese Philosophers: Ch'eng Ming-tao and Ch'eng Yi-ch'uan.* Lund, Humphries & Co., London, and Clarke, Irwin & Co., Toronto, 1958.

Heyerdahl, Thor. *The Kon-Tiki Expedition.* George Allen & Unwin, London, 1965. Rand McNally & Co., Chicago, 1968.

Hu Shih (1) "The Development of Zen Buddhism in China." *Chinese Political and Social Review,* vol. 15, no. 4. 1932.
(2) "Ch'an (Zen) Buddhism in China, Its History and Method." *Philosophy East and West,* vol. 3, no. 1. Honolulu, 1953.

Huang, Al Chung-liang. *Embrace Tiger, Return to Mountain: The Essence of T'ai Chi.* Real People Press, Moab, Utah, 1973.

Huyghe, René. *Art and the Spirit of Man.* Tr. Norbert Guterman. Harry N. Abrams, New York, and Thames & Hudson, London, 1962.

Kapleau, Philip, ed. and tr. *Three Pillars of Zen: Teaching, Practice, Enlightenment.* Harper & Row, New York, 1966.

Kepes, Gyorgy. *The Language of Vision.* P. Theobald, Chicago, and Alec Tiranti, London, 1945.

Legge, James, tr. *The Sacred Books of China: The Texts of Taoism.* Ed. F. Max Muller. 2 vols. Clarendon Press, Oxford, 1891. Repr., Dover Publications, New York, 1962.

Lin Yutang (1) *The Importance of Living.* William Heinemann, London, 1938. J. P. Putnam's Sons, New York, 1974.
(2) *The Wisdom of China and India.* Random House, New York, 1942. Michael Joseph, London, 1944, (2 vols.).
(3) *The Wisdom of Lao-tse.* Random House, Modern Library, New York, 1948.

Morgan, Evan. *Tao the Great Luminant.* Kelly & Walsh, Shanghai, 1934. Repr., Paragon Book Reprint Corp., New York, 1969.

Needham, Joseph. *Science and Civilization in China.* 5 vols. Cambridge University Press, 1954–74.

Radhakrishnan, Sarvepalli, tr. *The Bhagavadgita.* Harper & Row, New York, and George Allen & Unwin, London, 1948.

Reps, Paul. *Zen Flesh, Zen Bones: A Collection of Zen and Pre-Zen Writings.* Charles E. Tuttle Co., Tokyo and Rutland, Vt., 1957.

Rickett, W. Allyn. *Kuan Tzu.* Hong Kong University, 1965. Oxford University Press, New York and London, 1966.

Rose-Innes, A. C. *Beginner's Dictionary of Chinese-Japanese Characters.* 4th ed. International Publications Service, New York, 1973.

Rozin, Paul, Susan Poritsky, and Raina Sotsky. "American Children with Reading Problems Can Easily Learn to Read English Represented by Chinese Characters." *Science,* March 26, 1971.

*133*

Schwenk, Theodor. *Sensitive Chaos*. Tr. Olive Whicher and Johanna Wrigley. Rudolph Steiner Press, London, 1965.

Senzaki, Nyogen, and Paul Reps, trs. *The Gateless Gate, or Wu Men Kuan (Mumon Kan) by Ekai*. J. Murray, Los Angeles, 1934.

Siu, R. G. H. *The Man of Many Qualities: A Legacy of the I Ching*. M.I.T. Press, Cambridge, Mass., 1968.

Sze, Mai-mai. *The Tao of Painting*. Bollingen Series XLIX, 2nd ed. (2 vols. in 1). Princeton University Press, 1963.

Thoreau, Henry David. "Walking." In *Walden and Other Writings of Henry David Thoreau*. Random House, Modern Library, New York, 1950.

Waley, Arthur. *The Way and Its Power: A Study of the Tao Te-ching and Its Place in Chinese Thought*. George Allen & Unwin, London, 1956. Grove Press, New York, 1958.

Ware, James R., tr. *The Sayings of Chuang Tzu*. New American Library, Mentor Books, New York, 1963.

Watson, Burton, tr. *Complete Works of Chuang-tzu*. Columbia University Press, New York, 1968.

Watts, Alan (1) *Zen Buddhism*. Buddhist Society, London, and P. D. and Ione Perkins, Pasadena, Calif., 1947.
(2) *Zen* (same book as above, but enlarged). Delkin, Stanford, Calif.. 1948.

Welch, Holmes. *The Parting of the Way*. Methuen & Co., London, 1958. Beacon Press, Boston, 1966 (as *Taoism: The Parting of the Way*).

Whyte, Lancelot Law. *The Next Development in Man*. Cresset Press, London, 1944. Henry Holt, New York, 1948.

Wieger, Leon. *Chinese Characters: Their Origin, Etymology, History, Classification, and Signification*. Tr. L. Davrout. 2nd ed. 1927. Repr., Dover Publications, New York, 1965.

Wilhelm, Richard (1) *I Ching or the Book of Changes*. Tr. Cary F. Baynes. Bollingen Series XIX. 3rd ed. Princeton University Press, 1967.
(2) *The Secret of the Golden Flower: A Chinese Book of Life*. Tr. Cary F. Baynes. Rev. ed. Harcourt, Brace & World, New York, and Routledge & Kegan Paul, London, 1962.

Wittgenstein, Ludwig. *Tractatus Logico-Philosophicus*. Routledge & Kegan Paul, London, and Harcourt, Brace & Co., New York, 1922.

Yampolsky, Philip B., ed. and tr. *The Platform Sutra of the Sixth Patriarch*. Columbia University Press, New York, 1967.